Married Love

Married Love

An enquiry and a dialogue with his people

A Pastoral Letter by

Emile-Joseph de Smedt

Bishop of Bruges

Fides Publishers, Inc.
Notre Dame, Ind.

This pastoral letter was first published in 1963, under the title
L'Amour Conjugal, by Editions Ch. Bayaert, Bruges.
The English translation is by Jennifer Nicholson
© translation, 1964, Geoffrey Chapman Ltd.

Printing History

First Printing 1964
Second Printing 1966

Imprimatur: H. Gibney, *Vic. Gen.*
Nihil obstat: R. D. Dermitius Fogarty, D.D., L.C.L.,
censor deputatus
Datum Southwarci die 5a Augusti, 1964.

Printed in U.S.A.

Contents

CONTENTS

Preface

The Ecumenical Council has awakened in many of the
faithful the desire to dedicate themselves to the defence of
spiritual and moral values in modern society. They are asking
how they can make their action practical, and how they can
best work together with men of good will who are striving
for the same end.

My dear people, at the beginning of Lent I made a sug-
gestion to you. I drew your attention to the critical position
of family life today, and I proposed the organisation of an
extensive campaign to safeguard the peace and union of our
homes. I indicated a way to put this plan into practice which
will no doubt be the beginning of a new kind of collaboration
between Christian people and their Bishop. This was my
idea: the faithful should meet together, either in their own
homes or in small groups, to ask the help of the Holy Spirit
and to consider the forms of action which in present circumstances could best strengthen the unity of our homes; they
should then write to me, either individually or jointly, with
the result of their deliberations; I would myself study all their
letters, and finally, in a Paschal message to you all, sketch

the broad lines of a movement on a diocesan scale for the protection of the home.

This plan was warmly welcomed. For weeks, in widely differing circles and in countless families, the indissolubility of marriage and the dangers threatening it were discussed with great animation. You prayed, and you pooled the results of your inquiries and deliberations. There was no lack of suggestions. Replies poured in to me at a rate exceeding all expectations. At the lowest estimate, some 2,500 of the faithful took part in the composition of these letters. Thanks to all these kind collaborators, I have a mass of documentary evidence, together with thousands of suggestions and proposals, of great variety and practical value.

I am grateful to all who wrote to me. I am touched by the straightforwardness of their letters, their spontaneity and frankness, as well as by the sincerity with which their writers have confided their joys and sorrows to me and shown me the source of their happiness or the causes of their bitterness. I was deeply moved by the solicitude of all my correspondents for the happiness and well-being of their brethren. If they wrote to me, it was in the hope that their advice or suggestions might help to safeguard family life in this time of crisis.

The impression that first emerges from all this correspondence is of the complexity of the problems that beset our families nowadays, in our own region as well as everywhere else. Divorce is on the increase. Many couples who marry very young separate only a few months after the wedding. In other cases, after long years of life together, parents who find themselves at variance rush into divorce without a thought for the future of the children.

Nor is this distressing situation limited to the increase in the number of divorces. In some circles, adultery and unfaithfulness are the small change of daily life, so that some people are tempted to see them as an inevitable evil. Many young people no longer believe in marital faithfulness. The press, books and cinema do their best to encourage this deplorable attitude.

But these failures so openly admitted, these lamentable situations displayed in the full light of day, are not the only ones we have to consider. What are we to say about the deep-rooted unhappiness and the immense distress of many families where an outward show of faithfulness can barely conceal growing disharmony and disunion? Life in common amounts to very little in many homes—mere dormitories where co-habitation has become desperately anonymous and superficial! Husband and wife no longer have anything to bind one to the other, nothing to bring them together, and their actions and attitude are those of strangers. Even where good manners manage to avoid open quarrels, the void still exists, the slow, inexorable impoverishment and death of all sympathy, kindness and patient charity. The children unfortunately are the first to notice the impassable barrier which has imperceptibly grown up between their parents. If we are to sweep aside all the deceit and lack of understanding that has accumulated in the course of years in hearts and feelings, we need far more than a few belated attempts to safeguard this last appearance of harmony.

Our situation today is worse than alarming, and it requires a collective effort of thought. Every one of us, in his own station and as far as his responsibilities permit, must do his utmost to help where the need is greatest. We must find a remedy for the present crisis. And it is not enough to cure it. We must be able to prevent the evil spreading once more. A therapeutic of love is unthinkable without a prophylactic. What means must we use to attain our end?

And now, my dear people, you have before you the

summary of what hundreds of letters have suggested to me. I have tried to bring out the principal ideas which we can take as guides to action. Some of these ideas have already been put before you in the pastoral letter read from your pulpits. But I am not at the moment going to touch on the relations between parents and children within the home. There is so much material for this that I shall have to treat it in a separate booklet, which will probably be published under the title 'Understanding Parents'.

We are told that the first Christians 'had all things in common'. You present-day Christians have done the same. Now you have at your disposal the wealth of wisdom and experience accumulated by the whole diocese. Use this capital freely; what is new, take for your own enrichment, and what you already know, put more strenuously into practice in your own homes: *nova et vetera*.

This is my advice to you. Every evening, when the house is calm and quiet, take this little book and read a short extract from it. Do this in union of heart and mind with your partner, and even eventually with the older children. Discuss together what you have read. Drop by drop, its wisdom will sink in and increase your capacity for love. And the next day it will help you to work together more closely with all men of good will who, like you, are concerned to safeguard the unity of the home.

I

The Family in Danger

The family is a living cell in human society and in the Church. Like every other living organism, it has to defend its unity from dangers within and without. These were the two questions I asked in the course of our inquiry: *Have you observed, in the families round about you, any weakening or dissolution of the harmony between husband and wife? What steps should these couples have taken, in your opinion, to prevent the disaster?* On the basis of your answers I shall in this first chapter talk of the enemies without, against which every home must be forearmed and its defences prepared. I shall then show you what, within the home itself, are the disruptive elements which we must fight.

EXTERNAL DANGERS

A home must be itself. The sacramental bond that makes man and wife one, the affinities of blood and affection between parents and children, are founded on ties and relationships between persons. In no family could an outsider take the place of one of its members, whether as father, mother, son or daughter. Each member of a family is irreplaceable, each bears his own responsibility. The Lord gives to each the natural energy and the supernatural grace he needs to play his part within the family. In every home the father's love, the mother's, and the children's, has its own special character. Every mother has good reason to know the truth of the proverb: 'Like mother, like daughter.' Every family is made up of 'chips off the old block'. In every family too there are instinctive attitudes, relationships, ways of feeling and reacting which, taken together, are 'typical', characteristic of one family circle, and never exactly the same from one family to another. An outsider with any powers of observation and tact respects this state of things and avoids anything that could jeopardise the spontaneous and normal relationships which make up the fabric of family life.

Over-solicitude

One point that I find very striking is the number of correspondents who stress the need for every couple to have their own home from the very day of their wedding. All young people should be able to rent or own their own house or flat. It is unanimously agreed that living with the parents of husband or wife is unwise. Some letters quote the text from Genesis: 'A man shall leave father and mother, and shall cleave to his wife.'

A headmaster writes:

'Through observing children, a schoolmaster learns a great deal about family situations. Long years in teaching have given me a certain experience. May I tell you one thing I have noticed?

'Young couples who live with their parents-in-law, temporarily or permanently, do not—with rare exceptions— achieve their full development. When parents and married

*children live under the same roof they inevitably often come
into collision. The daughter is still under her parents' influence. At least so it seems to the husband, and he feels that
his parents-in-law stand in the way of his making his own
home. He has no standing. So he wants a limited number of
children, or no children at all. He is embarrassed by the
parents' presence and does not look into his wife's eyes. And
for man and wife to look into each other's eyes is not only
human, but necessary; it forestalls infidelity.*

*'In my opinion, this is a danger that the family must avoid.
Of course there are difficulties. The son or daughter lives with
the parents for a time. After they have saved a little money,
they build their own house. But meanwhile what has happened between husband and wife? Too often a deep rift has
opened up between them. As far as is humanly possible,
parents must let their children live by themselves.*

*'One other thing. The family should not interfere with the
young people. And by "interfering" I mean not the help that
one home can give the other, but the endless tittle-tattle: "My
daughter does this, my son-in-law does that."*

*'Let parents, brothers and sisters leave the young couple
in peace to build their own nest. If they need help, well and
good; but parents must see this as yet another opportunity
to show unselfish love. Any right-minded son or daughter
will be grateful for this attitude, and no loving father and
mother will pride themselves on it.'*

This conclusion resulted from an exchange of views between members of Strada and the Working Women's
League: [1]

*'If young couples live with their parents-in-law, they rarely
find true family happiness. They are always to some extent*

[1] Ligues Ouvrières Féminines.

under constraint. In the first stages of their marriage, when they still have to get used to one another, the tacit super-vision embarrasses them and they cannot feel really indepen-dent and at home. They have to go out to breathe freely and find relaxation. Fatal results soon follow: they get into the habit of living outside the home, they feel children are a nuisance, and materialistic ideas take root and end by des-troying all their conjugal life.'

Parents must get it into their heads that in being over-anxious for their children's happiness they err in their affec-tion. They must be careful to avoid any 'paternalistic' or 'maternalistic' attitude, and let their married children shoul-der their own responsibilities and follow their own tastes.

Parents must judge the attitude of each partner in the marriage quite objectively and impartially, and show each the same affection. By taking sides in any disagreement or mis-understanding, they run the risk of aggravating the quarrel. Their chief concern must be not to act as arbiter, but to en-courage mutual understanding and avert tactfully anything that endangers it.

This is what an 18-year-old student writes:

'I know a home where husband and wife cannot agree on the number of children. The wife, an only child, has always been spoilt by her mother, and still constantly goes home to her. I feel myself that the mother should have advised her daughter to put her difficulties to her husband simply and clearly. But what happens in fact is just the opposite: the mother sets her daughter against the husband, and he more and more seeks the company of certain of his friends. His wife is disgusted with him, and confides more and more in her mother. So the rift between them goes on growing wider. It's

a fine thing for a mother to sow discord in her daughter's home!'

A good many other letters tell of cases where parents influence their son or daughter to see things as they do—for example over the building of a new house, and many other things—and so often succeed in setting husband and wife at variance. I can only earnestly beg you to avoid this kind of ill-judged interference.

But a very proper wish to be independent does not absolve a young couple from the formal *duty* of respect and gratitude to their parents. These are feelings natural to right-minded children, and should gain strength as they grow in piety and begin to have a better understanding of the difficulties of parenthood. If you have reached a higher level, socially or intellectually, always remember that you owe it to those who brought you up. And never forget that the best way to see filial love growing in your own children is to practise what you preach.

Dangerous intimacy

The home must also protect its intimate life against friends and neighbours. 'We are neighbours' must never come to mean 'we are completely at home in your house'. Do not let anyone who is not of your family feel completely at home in its circle. When there is too much familiarity, bringing people too close together, the best friend of husband or wife becomes a danger. In this connection several correspondents point out that watching television together is not without risks.

A businessman writes:

'We regularly invite families with whom we are on friendly terms to watch television with us. After a few weeks one of our daughters, an 18-year-old, warned us of a very real danger.

This was perhaps our salvation. She told us: "I think that the intimate atmosphere, the half-dark, the proximity, sometimes heightened by what we are watching on the screen, isn't good for any of us." My wife and I discussed it frankly. Our eyes were opened.'

A section of the Christian Workers Movement[1] notes that *'if mutual understanding has disappeared from some respectable households, lack of forethought is to blame. Some religious observances were kept up in these homes, even if very superficially. They made their great mistake in being too friendly. Not a day went by without the same visitors dropping in to watch television. And in that familiar atmosphere of semi-darkness and silence, excessive intimacy gradually produced a false position. After a while no one has the courage to put an end to it. Harmony belongs to the past.'*

The enemy within our walls

Another factor threatening the inner life of the home is the omnipresence of mass-communication techniques, which harass us wherever we may be, through sound-waves, visual images or the printed word. In some programmes and publications laxity of conduct, infidelity and adultery are flaunted in the full light of day, shown as common practice and a matter of course. It is a paradoxical and highly dangerous situation, and few people are alive to it; the family is steeped from morning to night in an atmosphere, a prevailing tone, created by music-hall and theatre artists who are themselves deeply imbued with naturalism and irreverence for holy things.

Several correspondents assert that this field calls for a systematic campaign to open the eyes of the public.

[1] Mouvement Ouvrier Chrétien.

'*It is unworthy of educated people to submit passively to the brain-washing that the techniques of mass-communication bring into our very homes. Public authorities and influential bodies must certainly join forces to stop certain broadcasts that are undermining the foundations of family life. But also, in this society criss-crossed by opposing ideological currents, every individual must learn to take up his own personal and considered position. Above all, Christian families must be given the training that will allow them to play their part as adult Christians, and in full knowledge of the facts to take their stand before the problems raised by modern technical methods.*'

That is what a barrister says. He goes on:

'*In this field, the film discussion-groups that are being organised in many places, and the articles on cinema and radio in our newspapers and magazines, are doing a very real service. It is to be hoped that all our families will realise this, and appreciate the value of the various organisations holding the Bishop's mandate which strive to inform consciences and organise the apostolate in the fields of press, cinema, radio and television.*'

Another of our diocesans, also a doctor at law, has sent us this plea.

'Quousque tandem . . . *How far must the evil spread before a league is formed in this Christian province, and hundreds of thousands of Christians say bluntly to the radio producers and magazine editors: We've had enough of it! We are trying, not without difficulty, to preserve a Christian atmosphere in our homes, and you come and corrupt them with hysterical music, with songs which scoff at respect for love, women and the virtues of married life, songs whose currency is the crudest*

*naturalism, which uphold and glorify the most stupid and in-
ept forms of idolatry, which ridicule everything worthy of
veneration. It is not good enough to answer: You can always
switch off; for, as you know, radio, over-rated as it is, is a
necessity for young people nowadays; and what about the
millions you get from the taxpayers? Should they be used
to corrupt homes, and not rather to civilise and foster them,
to raise their standards spiritually, artistically, intellectually,
morally? If we are forced to organise this league, we hope
that similar leagues will come into being everywhere, and will
throw up a barrier against the maleficence of what ought to be
the tool of a higher civilisation.'*

Social events

We should be on our guard too against the abuse of a kind
of evening party which is very popular at the moment. In
some circles this is a truly tyrannous fashion. Its first victims
are the children. It is very harmful for a child not to feel at
night that the loving presence of his mother is at hand to
guard him, not to be able to fall asleep under the reassuring
protection of his father, the strong man who in his eyes knows
everything and can do everything. And what of those little
'hermits' who are left alone with instructions to 'be good' and
work at their books while their parents go out to have a good
time? But the parents as well easily become the victims of
these evening parties. Meeting the same people time after
time, in an atmosphere that stimulates the senses, becomes in
the end a danger for every husband and every wife.

*'Some parties, of the kind usual in our middle classes, are
very dangerous,' writes one of our correspondents. 'Several
households meet regularly at them. There would be no ground
for objection if the men discussed business together and the*

women confined themselves to domestic and house-keeping problems. But if a man regularly meets another man's wife at these parties, he will try to meet her during the day too. I speak from experience.'

On this subject, several correspondents comment very sensibly on the thoughtlessness and imprudence shown in the way some women appear at these parties or receptions. Indeed, while the men are irreproachably dressed, the young women slavishly follow fashion and come half-clad, in dresses that fall far short of real distinction. In their thoughtlessness —or their half-complicity—they pay little heed to the effect they produce on their friends' husbands, or to the temptations that beset their own husband in such surroundings. At some receptions it is a striking fact that women of the highest social class are far more correct and restrained in dress and behaviour than women of less exalted rank—who should find food for thought here. In these days we hear so much about 'promoting the cause of women'; will not Christian women come soon to be courageous and determined enough to refuse to tolerate and to imitate any fashion that does not respect feminine dignity and delicacy? How much longer will they let themselves be humiliated thus, and blindly collaborate in this lowering of moral standards? And how, in the secrecy of their own conscience, can they justify their connivance at what they cannot deny are shameful practices? Take care! The mad gaiety of some of these parties is often the beginning of tragedy.

After all, we must not imagine any of us are made of bronze or granite. Some correspondents stress this: it is easy to be deceived about people's qualities and charms when one does not have to share with them the worries of day-to-day life. One knows one's own wife only too well. . . . Sharing the same worries and responsibilities almost inevitably gives rise to disagreements, or at least to divergences of opinion over necessary decisions. People can be nervy, impatient, cross. There are clashes of temperament, and failings come out into the full light of day. One feels limited and imperfect, confronted by someone just as limited and imperfect. Imperfection in what one loves is painful, and demands patience and tolerance; all that is in the nature of things. But the man or woman one meets well away from any of the factors that make life complicated and cast shadows on it may seem to have none of these defects and shortcomings. Husband or wife is deceived into thinking they have found someone with all the gifts and qualities that are lacking in their partner, and with none of the failings.

Dangers in the office and factory

The same situations arise between employers and secretaries who must meet every day and work together in an unavoidable intimacy. As one letter says:

'*An employer of about 40 takes on a young saleswoman. Their intimacy develops gradually. The girl is so willing, has such a good head for business, is everything that could be wished for. Sales soar. Six months later there is a violent quarrel in the girl's family, and as a result she leaves home. Her boss is no hardened business man. He is sorry for her. He consults his wife, and they agree to offer the girl a home with them. He drives back with her every evening. The wife and the girl become great friends. The four children adore her—she is the perfect playfellow.... The bombshell bursts eight months later. It should be noted that this is the second time a home has been broken up by this young woman.*

Her method is always the same: she makes herself too well-liked by both wife and husband.'

Another correspondent stresses this point:

'Mutual understanding runs great risks when wife and children go away for the holidays without the husband. What is going on at home meantime? And here is another danger: the wife's undue familiarity with tradesmen: butcher, baker and milkman all call regularly while the husband is out. Loneliness and boredom are bad counsellors.'

One of the devil's favourite means of disrupting a household is that misleading and deceptive emotion, compassion. It all begins on such a high plane. You feel real interest in someone in trouble, and deep sympathy. You make no secret of your feelings. You want to give proof of your affection to show your compassion. At first no more than words are involved. But soon, if you are not careful, another kind of affection kindles in your eyes. A handshake over-prolonged, a light caress, and the fuse is ignited. Next time you meet, you go on a little further from there. Insidiously *caritas* becomes *carnalitas*.

A priest, and a good psychologist, very rightly points out:

'The tears of a third person are often the corrosive that destroys a home. Pity is highly inflammable, and should be kept well away from fire. It is always dangerous in a confined space.'

The place of work, if men and women are employed together, is a cause of moral ruin for many homes. This is especially true of the relations between inferiors and superiors. Withholding a worker's wage is a sin that calls aloud for vengeance; but the crime is more serious still and more shocking when the employer, the manager, or the foreman makes an attempt upon the liberty and moral integrity of a subordinate. This is scandalous abuse of a superior's authority over people who must be tempted by the fear of losing their job to accept a situation that their conscience condemns.

And here I am thinking of car drives where the car becomes a place of corruption. I am thinking of the profanation of the home, even of the marriage bed in the absence of the lawful husband or wife. I am thinking of public-houses whose unscrupulous owners force present-day slaves into actions from which their very soul shrinks.

In a wider field, I must speak out in defence of young people subjected to the whims of the influential. Some scoundrels are very well dressed. But they must not harbour any easy illusions: they it is whom Christ denounces when he says: 'He that shall scandalise one of these little ones . . . it were better for him that a millstone should be hanged about his neck and that he should be drowned in the depth of the sea' (Matt. 18: 6).

DANGERS WITHIN

Such are the dangers that threaten the unity of your homes from without; but you must also, my dear people, be alert and watchful against the inward causes of disunion. These can endanger everything in a home, from mutual understanding down to every value of education and sanctifying virtue that family life stands for.

Letters from young people point out the tragic results of love of money or the 'passionate' quest for comfort. And they express their indignation in very clear terms. Happily their idea of family life is a very different one.

'Some parents,' writes a girl, a student, 'insist on their children staying at home as long as possible to bring in money. The young people want to get married, or enter religion. Their parents exert pressure, or insist on their waiting another year to help pay for the new house. The next year the same tactics are employed, but this time for the new car or television, etc. The young people find this attitude more than they can bear; they break away from their parents, and at the same time lose their affection for their brothers and sisters. Love of money and luxury keeps them out of the home more and more. It kills family life. And what happens is that the members of a family like this, though still living under the same roof, end up as strangers to each other, and worse still stop loving one another.'

Obviously, to run a household and bring up children requires an adequate income. It is an elementary parental duty to work to this end. And it is natural that married couples should try to raise and improve their standard of living. Parents cannot be blamed for being thus far concerned with material progress; they would be failing in their Christian duty of forethought if they did not make provision for the future, or foolishly squandered what they have. Business-like and provident parents are a blessing to each other, as well as to their children. As soon as the children are of an age to earn, it is natural that they should help their parents, especially if there are still younger children to be brought up.

But married couples must go to the lengths of being so absorbed by material preoccupations that they neglect the moral and spiritual interests of their family. Here too the home must be itself. It is foolish to be influenced by the example of luxury and comfortable living in other homes and to struggle to equal them. Many families seem to forget that material well-being is not an end in itself, but only a means to achieve happiness in the home. Unfortunately they are hypnotised by the means, to such an extent that they have no time or attention to devote to the business of living their married life together as human beings, before God, in mutual love and self-sacrifice.

A priest, after a long spell in the Congo, expresses what a great many colonials feel:

'We exiled ourselves in the interests of our families, to secure a better future for our wives and children. And now what do we find? That our wives and children are the first victims of our mad venture.'

That should serve as a warning for many businessmen. They must take care not to end up by sacrificing wife and children to their interests! This is the experience of one employee:

'For some years I have been working overtime to add to my earnings. I come home at night tired out. How can a father take a proper interest in wife and children when he is utterly exhausted? This has gone on long enough. As soon as I possibly can I shall give up overtime work. What I want is a more regular family life. We shall take a little longer to resolve our material difficulties. I shall be content with a little less comfort, for comfort is no substitute for happiness in the home.'

This preoccupation with material possessions is seen not only in the frantic pursuit of wealth, but often in a use of leisure that is harmless in itself but not in the interest of wife and family. This letter tells a tragic story:

'A young couple, in complete harmony. Their life together is enriched by the arrival of their first child. They are

perfectly happy. The wife is glad to have a good husband who never goes out and finds all his happiness in the home. But there is a darker side to the picture—his books; he is anxious to study, to pass examinations, to improve his standard of living, for the sake of his family. He is a brain-worker. He sacrifices everything to his studies. His young wife would like to go out sometimes. He makes no objections. He's a good husband and doesn't mind his wife having a little entertainment! But he stays at home, with his son and his beloved books. He is completely blind to the needs of his young wife; and all she wants is a little home life with him, a heart-to-heart talk, a run in the car together. Later on, he thinks; for the time being, I've got to study. In her disappointment the young wife wanders aimlessly through the deserted streets. Deep in her heart is the wound through which her youth and gaiety are ebbing away.... The tragedy has happened. She has left her husband, and now he can only shed tears over all he has left of his former happiness—his little son Herman, three years old and abandoned by his mother.'

The mother's absence from home

Here we come up against the problem of working mothers. It is sometimes said ironically that for a woman 'marriage' means 'housekeeping', that the kitchen is the sanctuary where she must work out her salvation, as if a woman's horizon, once she is married, shrank to the cares and chores of the house. Against this point of view can be argued the woman's right to develop her full personality, to undertake paid work suitable to her capacities, and to play an effective part in public and cultural life.

It is impossible to lay down a general rule of conduct; every case is different. Obviously the unmarried woman, like a man, must be able to earn her living. This is not the place to discuss where woman is superior to man in the plane of divine wisdom, and where inferior. But one thing must be clearly understood: when a woman gets married, she accepts the rôle which, by virtue of the very institution of the family, falls to the wife and mother. From that moment onwards she cannot organise her life in a way that would interfere with the task she has shouldered in the home, and which she cannot delegate. She must use her woman's intuition to see that her household becomes a real 'home', drawing everyone to its atmosphere of peace and intimacy, warmth and understanding. On her falls, in the first resort, the responsibility for the care and upbringing of the children. The plight of motherless children shows us clearly what a mother means to a child. A home must never become a hotel, where people go just to eat and sleep. The first responsibility a woman accepts on her marriage is the responsibility of making the house a 'home' for each one of her family. That is the part she must play as a woman and a Christian: making sure that her husband and children have the moral and material elements they need for their fulfilment. And don't let us hear anything about the subordinate rôle of women! Is it not obvious that in this sphere the husband is the dependant, relying on the talents and self-sacrifice of his wife?

How far can this difficult task be combined with work outside the home? In each particular case husband and wife should examine the question very carefully together. They should come to a decision only after mature reflexion, and with all the caution the problem demands. There are undoubtedly cases where weighty considerations justify a wife's going out to work.

A family man writes:
'*The parish magazine has already published several articles*

on wives working outside the home. My wife is one of those who go out to work. She started when the children began to grow up. In the evening, after the day's work, we all lend a hand with the housework. The children are given little jobs that would otherwise fall on their mother. In this way boys and girls have a chance to familiarise themselves with household tasks; that in itself is educational. It is a great pity when the mother has to go out to work, but as things are in this country higher education puts parents to considerable expense. Some solution has to be found. These expenses cannot be met from the husband's salary. We chose the lesser evil, and my wife works in a college with a strong Christian tradition, where all, staff included, are women. Perhaps one day our children will thank us. Anyway, I can say, thank God—and we do thank him daily that our family is very united. Our children give us every satisfaction, and in spite of a few shadows on the picture we are very happy together. Trials, whether great or small, come to all of us. Though we have had our share already, family happiness is still with us.'

The problem of 'mother at home' is most difficult when the children are still very young. It is hard to see how the writer of the next letter could carry out her work as housewife and teacher so devotedly if she added to her commitments regular work outside the home.

'A woman must be entirely wife and mother. That is her first duty. And so it is essential, even if it sounds paradoxical, that she should be very careful about her health and her rest. If she is ill, tired, or nervy, she cannot create a serene and happy atmosphere. Further, she should take pains over her appearance, and every now and then read a serious book. She cannot neglect her spiritual life; she must take the sacrament as often as she can, and draw all her strength

*from the Lord. How can she 'bring up' her family if her
horizon is limited to housekeeping and dress? The influence
of a God-fearing, loving mother is indispensable in bringing
up children. And a mother can always find time to pray. While
she is washing up, preparing vegetables, and so on, she is
usually on her own and can talk with God in all simplicity
about her worries, her husband, her children. She must always welcome her husband with a smile and a pleasant word.
If he happens to come into the kitchen she should let him
see how pleased she is, and give him some fruit or titbit. And
she must always have time to listen to the children. When they
come in from school, mother must be at home. They come in
full of little bits of news to tell mummy. Sometimes too there
are squabbles, an understandable reaction after long hours
of application at school. Mother will let the storm pass, and
everything will be all right again at family tea. Sometimes
there are dull, grumpy days when the barometer drops very
low. That is the time to produce pancakes or waffles, and good
temper returns at once.*

'*It is important for a mother to be a good cook. Husband
and children come home eagerly when they know they will
be welcomed with a good meal. They must feel comfortable
and relaxed at home. There should not be too much fuss if
children come in with muddy shoes, or cigarette ash is
dropped anywhere but in the ashtray. Children must be able
to play and enjoy themselves, even if tidiness suffers a
little.*

'*The mother must also be careful to balance her budget,
not to be extravagant in the years of plenty or complain in
the lean years. Her husband must realise that his work is
appreciated and that what he earns is judiciously spent.*

'*As the eldest of my children is only nine, I cannot speak
from experience about gaining the confidence of adolescents.*

But I can say what I am doing now to deserve their confidence later on. I begin when they are very young—being a child myself with them, chatting, playing, singing, and so on. Later I tell a lot of stories, and above all listen a lot. So a mother can if necessary put right misconceptions, guide a child towards loving his neighbour, and so on.

'Bringing up children demands complete dedication. I notice that my younger children are less highly-strung, more lovable and more open than the older, no doubt because when the first were born I lacked the degree of detachment and unselfishness I have attained after eleven years of marriage. Perfection does not come all at once, it has to be striven for every day.

'And parents should not be too severe. Children must have a certain amount of freedom, and feel that they are being trusted. The mutual love of husband and wife is another important factor in children's trust in their parents.'

To come back to married women working outside the home, I have already said that one cannot lay down any absolute rule on this subject. The pros and cons must be carefully weighed, and the problem exactly formulated: is it absolutely necessary or desirable for the welfare of the family that the wife and mother should be regularly out of the house? Do the advantages outweigh the disadvantages?

It would be short-sighted and wrong to consider the material advantages alone. If there are serious reasons why the wife should work, then care must be taken that her work is not unhealthy or too tiring for a wife and mother. Only very weighty reasons can justify a mother's employment a long way from home, or her coming back at night to finish her work at home. And a wise couple will never on any account consent to her working in an environment that may be a moral danger to her. In short, before coming to any decision, husband and wife must approach the question with great prudence, and take advice from competent persons. And above all remember to pray for the guidance of the Holy Spirit!

Be careful what you say

The inevitable friction between two temperaments demands a great deal of patience and mutual understanding in husband and wife. There are moments in married life when you must remember that though words may be silver, yet silence is golden.

One of our correspondents tackles this question very sensibly:

'Be careful what you say! Many couples could have avoided countless difficulties by following this advice. Let them think over the subjects of the disagreements that have cropped up in their married life. Was there really any reason to get worked up over them? In a good many cases they won't even be able to remember the cause of the quarrel. What they will remember, though, are the offensive things they said. If only they had held their tongue when they realised that the quarrel was getting serious!'

An elderly correspondent says:

'I can easily forget the thoughtless words of my husband which have sometimes hurt and vexed me. What I cannot forget are his taunts in moments of anger. I forgive him, but I think I shall always remember them. His gibes have wounded me too deeply.'

Indeed, conversation plays an extremely important part in family life. A priest who has lectured a great deal on married life has sent me his notes. I feel I must quote some of his very sensible points:

'1. *Don't dramatise a simple difference of opinion or a characteristic that you find irritating. No two people in the whole world have exactly the same views on everything. But does this really matter? We all have our eccentricities. Why not put up with each other's? When something provokes or annoys you, ask yourself calmly if it is really essential for everything to be the way you want it.*

'2. *Don't be always dwelling on the same complaints. Harping on the same grievances only produces pointless quarrels and tiresome repetitions. The strongest nerves won't stand it!*

'3. *After some slight disagreement, don't take refuge in hostile silence. To show one's displeasure by an obstinate refusal to talk is childish, and would be quite ridiculous if it were not tragic. Just think of a married couple, living side by side and not speaking to each other! Two adults behaving like sulky children, each waiting for the other to break the ice! The longer it lasts, the more obstinate they get. Which of them is right? Neither, for both are wrong to persist in their stubborn silence. Don't be unreasonable; talk over your difficulties frankly. The wiser of the two will be the first to say, "I'm sorry, forgive me". Never go to sleep without making it up.*

'4. *Never harbour thoughts of revenge. Husband and wife should look at their difficulties together, simply and honestly. Otherwise their animosity builds up and runs the risk of developing into rancour and vindictiveness. At the critical moment, a mere trifle can kindle anger, and harsh, cruel words pass that jeopardise the unity of the home.*

'5. *At all costs, avoid saying anything to hurt or reproach your partner in public. There are some married people who, instead of giving pleasure by bringing out their partner's good qualities, are apt to be critical and sarcastic in the company of strangers, members of the family, and even, unfortunately, their own children. The pitcher that goes often to the well in the end is broken!*

'6. Don't live your lives on a war footing. Some people are well aware that attack is always the best form of defence. To any criticism by their partner they reply by another. And that starts up an endless quarrel!

'7. Be tactful and guarded in talking of each other's family. On this subject married people are very touchy. The slightest ill-judged word can strike a spark that may destroy your love. If in a quarrel one partner tries to wound the other by speaking slightingly of the other's family, the wound inflicted may be incurable.

'8. Finally, married people should be discreet. They should be able to confide to each other everything that is in their mind. Parents-in-law need not know about the minor clashes that are inevitable in the life of the home. Neighbours and acquaintances, who are often curious, must never penetrate to the inner sanctum of your family life. Nor can strangers be involved with it.'

Failure to help one another

Married life can be harmonious only if husband and wife try to know and understand each other's worries. In moments of difficulty they should help each other out in their work.

Serious difficulties often arise because the wife does not realise how much trouble and contrivance is required of her husband if he is to provide an adequate income for his family. She doesn't know the value of money, and wastes it on trifles or useless luxuries. Some women let themselves be guided by their fancies, and are hypnotised by publicity and good window-dressing. They do not stop to discuss with their husband whether certain out of the ordinary purchases are expedient, or whether their financial means can afford them. I have had sad and bitter letters from husbands who find it impossible to lead a happy life in a united family because the wife cannot keep her desires within bounds, and is constantly presenting her husband with a *fait accompli*. Many businesses have gone downhill, many houses have lost their peace, because of an extravagant wife.

'I have a perfect wife,' writes a wholesaler. 'She takes a great interest in my work and business. She never interferes with the management side, but concerns herself with sales and turn-over. At school she was good at mathematics, and I make full use of this! She consoles me when I am worried, and shares my gratification when I can book a substantial order. I find real satisfaction in keeping her informed of the general progress of my business, and asking her advice and the support of her prayers when I have to take an important decision. If I am overworked, she helps me out, in the evening with accounts and correspondence. She knows how much trouble I go to to provide her with the money she needs for household expenses. And the way she manages is nothing short of miraculous! On our limited income she contrives to feed and clothe our large family, to keep our home attractive and comfortable. And she manages all that without making any mystery of it. I tell her how my business stands financially, she talks to me about her budget. Through my contacts in business and private life, I know the difficulties other households have. I cannot thank God enough for such a wife!'

The husband on his side must take just as much interest

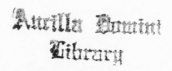

in his wife's work. Many women are embittered and suffer in silence because their husbands don't take them seriously and give them so little credit for the often exhausting work that fills their whole day. I should like all husbands to work out this little sum. When you have time, gentlemen, perhaps in the evening after your eight hours' work, or in the two days you have off at the end of the week, add up the hours of work, by the day and by the week, that your wife undertakes in the home. In many households, the so-called 'head of the family' is a 'gentleman' who lets himself be waited on without a word of thanks, without ever wondering if his wife is tired, and without even thinking that he might help with the housework now and then. Have men of this kind really no thought to spare for anyone but themselves? Do they ever think how distressing it is for a wife to find herself press-ganged into a life-time of serving her husband's selfishness?

A widow, sadly recalling the stages of her married life, writes:

'By my husband's death-bed I asked his forgiveness and I forgave him, and I pray every day that God will give him everlasting happiness. Nevertheless, I feel my life has been a failure. Love was dead in me, quite dead. Ill, pregnant, exhausted, I still had to get through my work. . . . And in spite of my ceaseless toil, I never had a word of encouragement, or a helping hand when I was expecting a baby, or one of my five children was ill. He even struck me if I dared to complain. Grief had destroyed love in me. I was at the end of my tether, worn out by work, but even more by grief, lack of understanding, and injustice. And in spite of everything I was careful about my appearance and kept our house clean and neat. A woman can do so much, and she is prepared to do it all, as long as she has encouragement and sometimes a little help in

her work. Otherwise her life, hard at the best of times, becomes unbearable, the conjugal act is just one more unpleasant duty, and she feels herself no better than a slave. This letter is not dictated by any spirit of bitterness against my dead husband. By the grace of his Christian death, our love has been reborn in Christ. But I write so that you may bring home to husbands how painfully many women are situated, and ask them to respect their wives and now and then give them a helping hand too. My time is over. My life is broken. I pray that my experience of unhappiness may be the salvation of other homes!'

A life of sin

But the greatest threat to the family today is sin. In every married couple, man and wife are still frail creatures on the brink of concupiscence. The law of God is the road that leads to peace and happiness, but it is sometimes very difficult to live by this law. Today's general atmosphere of immorality, in many cases combined with illness, weariness, cramped living quarters and lack of money, confront married couples with serious difficulties and painful temptations in their obedience to the Lord's holy law.

Those who honestly do their best to follow this law can count on God's help. The Father of mercy will not abandon men of good will who have been weak or are in a tight corner. Their heart is sound, even if some of their actions are reprehensible. The Lord is always ready to hear their sincere contrition, to forgive their sins in the sacrament of penance, and to strengthen their good intention by the bread of the Eucharist. Some years ago, in a pastoral letter called 'Marriage',[1] I showed how Christians in their moral difficulties can make God's law their life and find his peace. The more than

[1] *Le Mariage*, Pastoral letter, ed. Lannoo, Tielt.

500,000 copies of this booklet sold have perhaps brought comfort or help to homes beset by difficulties.

It is very different with married couples who have made deliberate choice of evil. For no valid reason they withhold the willing co-operation that the Master of Life requires in their marriage. They do not hesitate to make of their most intimate relations as it were a systematic refusal. When this is their attitude, physical union must inevitably undermine the unity of their marriage little by little and destroy family happiness. How could it foster and sustain love and fidelity if it never finds fulfilment in the complete serenity and self-surrender, the entire self-giving, which is nature's ardent wish? One can only pray that they may in the end come to understanding, that Christ will show them that marriage 'doesn't work' without generosity and a love of life.

2

The Foundations
of Christian Marriage

REAL LOVE

Where then are we to look for the deep-rooted *cause* of
the difficulties so common in our homes? All the answers we
have had agree in thinking that the deterioration of good
relations between husband and wife is almost always due to
failure to appreciate the nature of real love.

*'You must stress this point,' writes a correspondent from
the deanery of Popinghe. 'Real love, like a rare plant, needs
constant care. Without it, the plant dies for ever.'*

And a mother from Courtraisis follows on:

*The reason why there are so many unsatisfactory homes is
that people don't know how to love. That is a surprising thing
to say, when you have only to switch on the radio to hear
talk of love. The word has been degraded. We must re-learn
how to love.'*

This, I feel, is a very helpful diagnosis. If we want to restore the situation, every one of us, in his own circle and with
all the resources he commands, must set to work to

disseminate more accurate and more penetrating ideas on married love.

And as a beginning, young people who are engaged or newly married must be careful not to think of the attraction that belongs to instinct and the senses as the essence of love.

Certainly, they will find everything in marriage that delights the senses or gratifies their feeling a most valuable help, ordained by the Creator to enrich man and make it easier for him to fulfil his destiny. This spontaneous affection prompts young people to make light of anything in their partner that might hinder the fusion of their two lives. Love is blind, says the proverb. But there is a time-limit to this providential blindness. Sooner or later comes the moment of disenchantment, and the behaviour of one partner becomes a real test of the other. Weaknesses and imperfections, faults and failings, illness and setbacks of all kinds, bring the couple suddenly back to earth. For love and marriage, passion left to itself is not a good enough guarantee. If man and wife can meet only on the plane of physical and sentimental satisfaction, they will soon find themselves having to face the void of boredom or the bitterness of disappointment. Is not that the drama at the heart of so many homes nowadays?

But don't misunderstand me. The attraction of the senses is not intended to wither and die as soon as the honeymoon is over. On the contrary. It should, as married life goes on, increase, transcend itself, grow ever richer. Freshness of impressions and feelings, an eternal youthfulness of heart, are the priceless privileges of married life, blending two souls into one to love God and those God loves. There is nothing to equal this youthfulness. Look about you, and be glad for this spirit of youth fostered by a shared spiritual life.

And always be on your guard, that the vernal freshness which will naturally cling to the time of betrothal may survive and be perpetuated through the years. But note this carefully: from the first moment of meeting, you must lift your mutual attraction on to a higher plane and begin to give it the more refined, mysterious riches of real love.

What then does real love look like in all its purity and truth, this love which the whole world should see in your example and witness?

A teacher in a technical college describes it thus:

'Of course,' he says, 'my wife and I have our faults, but our affection is so deep and sincere that we scarcely notice them. Without conscious effort, each of us dwells only on the qualities of the other. Mutual kindness brings its own reward. But do away with love for one moment, and you can see no good except in yourself, and all kinds of frailties and imperfections in the partner you once loved.' And he adds shrewdly: *'In the long run, the only true wealth is the power to give. To give, to give oneself, spontaneously and unstintingly, is the character of love. And only at that price can true happiness be bought.'*

Now we know where we are. Real love can exist only if the married couple, guided by their deep attachment to God and constantly renewing their good intention, strive to help one another towards that full self-realisation which is the essential condition of joy and happiness. The married partner who continues enamoured of the other holds back nothing from the service of love. His whole mind, his will, heart and body, are set to gratify the loved one, encompassed by all the warmth of inward life. 'What can I do that my beloved may bring all his capacities to full flowering and so achieve happiness?' That is the profoundly human question that real love asks itself every moment of its life.

But many people go about thinking that love is a spontaneous, effortless emotion. We cannot too often repeat that real love is something quite different—the wonderful reward that crowns an unwearying effort of will. Husband and wife, they say, are pupils in the school of love. But schooling implies concentration and persevering effort. Married people must train themselves to detachment and self-forgetfulness. They are ready to take the risk of abandoning the search for happiness, and will find in the end that it is restored to them a hundredfold, more lovely and abundant than ever before, in the happiness of their partner. They learn that only patience and perseverance can build that kind of happiness. . . . Many of my correspondents point out that the love between married people should have the same characteristics, both attractive and exacting, as the supernatural love which St Paul extols in his Epistle to the Corinthians. You all know his hymn to charity: 'Charity is patient, is kind; charity envieth not, dealeth not perversely, is not puffed up; is not ambitious, seeketh not her own, is not provoked to anger, thinketh no evil; rejoiceth not in iniquity, but rejoiceth with the truth; beareth all things, believeth all things, hopeth all things, endureth all things. Charity never falleth away . . .' (1 Cor. 13:4-8).

Service—that is the password of real love—real love that will never seek its own profit by extortion concealed beneath words of flattery. Love is the servant, not the master. It seeks out the lowest place, holding it to be the best. Whoever lives by the light of that love can bear witness of himself, in the words of his divine Master: 'I am not come to be ministered unto, but to minister' (Matt. 20:28).

By what signs, then, can husband and wife know that their love is genuine? By the constant kindliness of each for the other, by the fact that in the little things of daily life as well as in the great they bend all their ingenuity to serve the love that makes them one, helping one another to bring all their talents to full flower, to reach the peaks of joy, happiness and holiness—so many letters have said this—which God has prepared for them as man and wife.

Henceforward, as I travel through the towns and villages of my diocese, I shall know that blessed homes are not the exception—homes where, amid the bustle of daily life, husband or wife interrupts work for a moment and murmurs a short heartfelt prayer of thanks to God for all the gifts they have been given in their partner.

Here is what a young working woman writes to me from the deanery of Avelgem:

'I never had any grounding in religion in my home. I was still very young when I went into the factory. My parents didn't get on together, so that I had very little to take with me in the way of spiritual luggage. Then I married a young man from a Christian home. That was a kind of rebirth for me. I couldn't understand how God could be so good as to bring a boy of that sort into my life. I have no hesitation in saying that in my dear husband I find every day the tangible proof of God's love for me. And I shall try in my turn to instil trust in that love into my children.'

Surely, dear people, the most valuable help we can give those round about us is to let them catch from us, if I may so put it, the infection of the hope that gladdens our hearts and the courage that strengthens us in time of trouble? We must proclaim from the housetops the message that married Christians can rely on something more than their own good intentions or their own strength in the long and beautiful apprenticeship of charity between husband and wife. And let it be our care from the beginning to confer on this charity the dignity of a profoundly human art, a mission of the spiritual order, and a vocation both exacting and exalted. Betrothed and newly married couples are necessarily only novices in this art. And unfortunately many of them, after years of marriage, have lost none of the clumsiness and inadequacy of beginners. Let them listen carefully to the testimony of this commercial traveller from Ostend, the father of five children.

'We have been married for seventeen years, seventeen years of deep happiness, in spite of the trials, both great and small, which we have not been spared. When I got married, I knew all the theory; I have done my best since then to put it into practice. I can never thank Providence enough for the perfect wife at my side, entirely understanding, eager to help me in my desire to become an instrument in the Lord's hands worthy of his love. Every morning I find him in the Eucharist and draw from him the strength I need to serve my profession well, and to grow and perfect myself in my calling as a husband. From Christ I have drawn strength for renewed effort every time a defeat or set-back has tempted me to lose courage or to give up. For however well we mean, we are still human!

'More than once illness and tribulation have invaded our home. Sometimes it was an effort to smile and be kind and patient. Five times my wife went through the long, painful months of waiting for her child to be born. Often, after an exhausting day, I had to lend a hand in the evening with the household chores. And then came the still more distressing time of my wife's long and serious illness. We both strove to see the hand of God in our sufferings, for the Lord tries the loyalty of those who call themselves his friends. And from the crucible of suffering our love emerged purified, and the *unity of our marriage strengthened, far beyond anything we could have achieved in happiness.*

'I sometimes find myself remembering what our love was in the first year of our marriage, and when I compare that with what it is now, I am surprised to find so much on the credit side. Suffering and trials work miracles. To genuine love they bring a purity, depth, loyalty, and devotion to the apostolic cause, that can be found nowhere else. That is why I give thanks to the Lord daily, realising how exceptional is our happiness.'

My dear people, you will not often hear those around you speaking of love in these terms. In our present-day world such a conception of love is regarded as fair game for mockery, or as proof of inconsistency. Magazines, novels, radio and music today preach an entirely different kind of gospel. They present everything as if the only aim in life were the pursuit of sensual enjoyment. In this pernicious atmosphere, we Christians must take up a courageous attitude in what concerns ourselves and our brethren, and repeat unwearyingly: 'Don't build your happiness upon sand.' Separating the carnal from the spiritual dehumanises it. As soon as sex ceases to serve love and the harmonious self-fulfilment of the married couple, it leaves man unsatisfied and discontented; it cannot contribute to his happiness.

At this moment I have in front of me hundreds of other letters from happy people, and almost all of them echo this theme:

'As Christians, we cannot go on keeping silence. We must speak out to all those whom life has disappointed, or failure embittered and driven to despair. We must show them the road that leads to the Christian solution of their problems, and pray that they may all one day taste of the inexpressible

joy God has prepared for all who answer his call with their whole heart, and sincerely try to apply his teaching in their married life—the teaching that uplifts and liberates them.'

Yes, dear people, we must hesitate no longer. We cannot be indifferent to the fate of those who have not found what they hoped for in their marriage. In all modesty, and in all readiness to share what we have with our brethren, we must concern ourselves with their happiness. There is still hope for them all: the hope of a new spring, a new life with the risen Christ, who has given us all the example of a life that finds fulfilment in self-giving and self-forgetfulness.

UNITY AND INDISSOLUBILITY

Love in marriage is genuine only in so far as the married couple is firmly resolved to persevere in their union until death, and to defend it from every attack from without. Four words, surprisingly simple words, are the foundation of community in marriage: *Only you, for ever.* Without unity and indissolubility there is no true marriage.

On this point, the conceptions current nowadays in our over-credulous and sensation-seeking public are completely discordant. So often the indissolubility of marriage is regarded as a tyrannical law, imposed from without, or simply as a ban on the unfaithfulness that is decked out in all the charms of forbidden fruit! Things have gone so far that a whole vocabulary of misused terms has been invented to plead this cause, and the magic of words threatens to disturb our mind and pervert our conscience. Films and novels describe the marriage bond as a chain fettering the fulfilment of husband and wife. In the imagination of many writers, the community of marriage has become a hell, where two creatures are chained together, their love extinguished, and reduced to hating and torturing one another in an eternal confrontation.

What can we do to throw light on this problem and influence public opinion? How can we help those around us to see more accurately and judge more soundly the deep realities of marriage? The present situation calls for an effort of thought, a conscious search for the essential kernel of married life. Only if married people themselves discover the deep meaning of their union and the dynamic character of their faithfulness as a mutual and life-long acceptance can they gradually build up a true community of love on the foundations of their common life. These are the views we must bring young people to adopt, if we are to help them to penetrate the mystery of Christian marriage.

In making this mental effort, every aspect of the indissolubility of marriage must be seen as an expression of the compact between married people, called to community of life and love. Marriage is in its very essence a work to be accomplished, a mutual compact to be constantly renewed. It is not the end but the birth of a genuine, lasting love, which must grow and deepen if it is not to die.

1. To illustrate the indissoluble nature of the community of man and woman in married life, we may begin with psycho-social considerations. More than ever before, thanks to recent work in psychology and sociology, the indissoluble unity of marriage is seen as an indispensable element in a healthy society.

We must first of all lay constant stress on the tragic consequences for the children of disagreement and disunion between husband and wife. The havoc caused is obvious to anyone; it is only too easily seen in our society, where the problems of mods and rockers and unemployed teenagers is the order of the day. How pathetic are the children of parents who do not make *'Only you, for ever'* an integral part of their life!

Think of all that society must do to help these forsaken young people. And yet the stability of marriage is a necessity not only for the young, their physical development and their growth to moral and mental maturity. The complete and life-long union of husband and wife is one of the essential conditions of harmony in our society. The personal value of married people can find fulfilment and recognition only if their giving implies and consecrates a union sealed for life.

2. But we must not stop at psycho-social considerations if we want to stress fully the indissoluble nature of the union of husband and wife. This indissolubility is not a law arrived at by deductions from apparent facts. It must be considered as an essential requirement of the love between man and wife whose one desire is the total giving of each to other. This is brought out by a philosophical reflexion on the phenomenology of married love. Love between husband and wife leads naturally to union of body, heart and soul. Its eager desire is genuine community, perfect harmony at all levels of human existence. It is essentially directed towards total self-giving, which finds its expression and fulfilment in the conjugal act. Let me put this question to all married people: When in perfect harmony you give yourselves each to the other in a spontaneous outburst of love, is not your union, at once spiritual and physical, the expression and consecration of the covenant sealed between the two of you by your 'I will' in the sacrament of marriage? What meaning, what scope, has your 'I will' in those moments of ardent union, if not the meaning we have just mentioned: *'Only you, for ever'?* That is the normal way, that is what is written into the very nature of the union of man and wife. Unity and indissolubility are the essential properties of marriage. They must be recognised

as such by the conscience of men. If married people come together without the firm intention of staying together in exclusive and lasting love, what are they doing but lying to each other? And both soul and body share in their insincerity. At such moments both are in league against the imperious dictates of conscience.

Because love between man and wife leads to physical union and boundless community, it cannot be compared with any other form of love. Parental love, even friendship, can grow wider and deeper as the family grows, or the circle of friends expands. But married love seeks to establish a true community of love between one man and one woman. It can come to its full flowering only if this community is definitive, for it bears on the uniqueness of a person growing to personal fulfilment at every level, and it supposes total involvement of both partners for life.

Only such involvement, without limit or restriction, allows husband and wife to accomplish the mission implied in their mutual love. And that love will find its fulfilment only in lifelong community.

That, then, is the positive meaning of faithfulness as an essential requirement of marriage.

A teacher in higher education writes:

'There is no sense in the objection: "What can marriage mean when love is no longer there?" The rôle of marriage is to initiate married couples in the art of loving, and help them to cultivate and deepen their love. Marriage goes beyond the anonymity of desire and the ebb and flow of passion because it is self-giving, without reserve or return, to the partner one has promised to love with heart, soul and body, in a union for better or for worse. Faithfulness in marriage is the condition, the expression, and the realisation of genuine

love, which desires always to be complete, and so exclusive and lasting.'

Faithfulness is essentially a task to be accomplished, a call to freedom, an invitation to involvement and responsibility. Marriage is in its essence a contract which is part of the mystery of human existence. In some measure it goes beyond the person of husband and wife; through marriage is formed a new unit and a new entity (the one flesh of Genesis), that only the total and free gift of husband and wife can bring to its full flowering.

3. The full meaning of faithfulness in marriage can be understood only in the light of a theological reflexion on marriage as a sacramental reality, the symbol and efficacious sign of the union between Christ and his Church.

That is the thought in the mind of the teacher just quoted when he stresses the religious basis of faithfulness in marriage.

'The mission of husband and wife is extremely exacting; it supposes an ever-growing will to self-sacrifice, and a dedication to unselfishness taken to ever greater lengths. Only married people who have penetrated the mystery of union in marriage can surrender themselves with rapture to what becomes for them the supreme realisation of themselves in self-giving and self-forgetfulness. But total giving is fully achieved, and the virtue of self-surrender gradually acquired, only when husband and wife have effective faith in the living God. For God himself is present at the heart of this mystery, because he is the source of all true love.'

The same conclusion was reached by a group of woman welfare-workers, who sent me their impressions after considerable experience of home-visiting.

'When a home is united,' they write, 'it is almost always because a truly Christian spirit permeates it. Prayer and trust in God always overcome difficulties, whether great or small. In houses like these, behind husband and wife one can glimpse the face of Christ.'

In Christian marriage, faithfulness is not a purely human achievement, due chiefly to the endeavours and efforts of husband and wife. Through the sacrament of matrimony, Christ has pledged himself to the married couple. He has bound himself by the most intimate links with their home, and is henceforward its chosen guest and intimate friend. The community of husband and wife, with all its inward life and its exteriorisations, is raised by his presence to the level of supernatural realities. But are you, I wonder, all you married Christians, fully aware of what that means for you? The grace of your marriage is infinitely more than an antidote to save you from the unfortunate consequences of human frailty! It is nothing less than the active *presence* of the divine Master at the very heart of your home—his supreme presence, ever to be adored, transfiguring your love and endowing with superhuman beauty, superhuman purity, the joys that lie at the heart of your community in marriage. Do you fully realise that through this divine presence your married love, even in its most intimate expression, *passes from its purely human dimension to the supernatural,* and that the significant acts of this love acquire thereby a completely new compass? So you have it in your power to glorify God in your love, and are able, through the sublimation of your community of husband and wife, to play your part in the redemptive mystery, the sanctification of the Bride of Christ, the Church. Do you realise that God's grace comes to strengthen your union and set the final seal on it? By a mysterious virtue of language, the word 'grace' evokes and implies the idea of charm and lovableness. So the grace of Christ shines upon you as husband or wife, and makes you still more attractive and lovable in the eyes of your partner. And as this grace casts its spell increasingly on your eyes and hearts, so your union becomes more complete, more intimate, more delightful.

Christian husbands and wives, if you approach in humility and in trust Christ present in your homes, if you drink deep of the inexhaustible springs of his grace, your community will be brought into the mystery of the Church, and cannot fail to grow ever deeper, and approach ever nearer to perfect communion in the love of the Father.

That is the gist of this letter from a director who has a large family.

'It is good,' he writes, that husband and wife should be aware of the presence of a Third. Christ has made his dwelling in their home. He it is who from all eternity has predestined them to know each other, and has brought their two destinies together, sometimes quite contrary to what could have been foreseen. From the moment of betrothal he has joined himself to the young couple, helping each to discover the other's qualities and endowments and to overlook failings, even as he in his kindness forgets our faults and frailties. Before the altar he binds himself finally to them. Christian marriage, as we see it, is on the spiritual plane a three-fold union. From the moment that the married couple shut out the person of the Third from their intimacy, their union is broken and torn apart. And yet reconciliation will always spring in his heart, whose love is the strongest and most faithful of the three. Then the miracle of rediscovery comes about, which sometimes no one could have dared to hope for, let alone predict.'

If this is really the inner nature of marriage, on both the

natural plane and the plane of grace, it is obvious that the Church can never in any circumstances countenance the dissolving of a marriage that has been freely contracted in her presence and consummated by the total self-giving of husband and wife in the conjugal act. The claim that the Church can in certain cases be bribed into dissolving the marriage bond is a lie and a slander. Remember what she has suffered, in the course of her history, because she would not yield on this point to the behests of the princes of this world. We must see that public opinion is informed, and constantly reminded that the Church can in no circumstances dissolve a Christian marriage that has been consummated. In only two cases can she intervene: (1) when after searching examination it appears that no conjugal bond has ever existed. In this case, the Church simply *states the facts* and declares officially that a union which seemed valid was not valid in reality, and had never been so, because it was null and void, and never existed; (2) when it is conclusively proved that a marriage has not reached full completion in the conjugal act. In this case, a special dispensation of the Sovereign Pontiff can, for serious reasons, dissolve the marriage bond.

Faced with the modern crisis, we must venture to ask whether the levity with which some baptised Christians talk of the indissolubility of marriage, and their foolhardiness in exposing their own community in marriage to inevitable dangers, are not the tragic result of a completely inadequate religious upbringing. And is not this lack of upbringing behind the despair and pessimism that gnaws at so many hearts nowadays? Are we careful to see that husbands and wives are fully aware that marriage only 'works' if it is sustained by prayer and trust in Jesus Christ? Have we really brought it home to married couples that marriage is a sacrament? And have we now emphasised strongly enough the fervour and energy that Christian husbands and wives should draw from their conviction that Christ is ever beside them to back up all their efforts? And finally, must we not recognise in the present day situation all the symptoms of an acute form of spiritual and religious under-development?

I am led to formulate all these questions by the writers of scores of letters insisting that a renewal of life and spirituality in marriage can only bear fruit to the extent to which Christian husbands and wives are aware of the dignity of their union as a sacrament of Christ and the Church. They never spoke a truer word! And it is the great merit of the various societies that foster the spiritual side of married and family life (and especially of the *Equipes Notre-Dame*), that they help their members not only to rediscover this truth but to bring all their ways of thought and action into line with it. And the educational sections of our Christian social organisations and our Catholic Action movements have also done fine work in this field.

My dear people, the particular grace of marriage, like every sacramental grace, will be fully efficacious only if the married couple really let Christ into their home, welcome his sanctifying action, and eagerly desire his help and presence. If they do this, the community of their marriage becomes communion with Christ.

The difficulties involved in the first stages of this community, the sacrifices implied in mutual self-giving, the trials inherent in the building of a home and family, are all invitations to share in the work of redemption in communion with the Lord. The faithful must be fully aware that through their baptism they participate in the death and resurrection of Christ. They must know that their incorporation in Christ means too that they are called upon to share the life of the Church and her mission, to obtain the salvation

of all men. In the light of this vocation and in the consciousness of their election, married Christians will come to full
understanding of the deep meaning of their consent. Their
mutual compact is a compact with God in the Lord. The
faithfulness that gives reality to this mutual consent for life
is a realisation of the Covenant between God and man in the
Lord. That is the deep-lying meaning of faithfulness, the
last foundation on which is built the indissoluble union of
marriage. Faithfulness is both the expression and the realisation of the consent exchanged between God and man;
marriage in Christ is the sacramental covenant on which the
whole structure of the Church is founded.

All those who have written to me are agreed, thank God,
that marriage cannot be lasting and happy without prayer and
grace. At least ninety per cent of the letters that have reached
me insist, directly or indirectly, on the necessity for husband
and wife of humble, trusting prayer. It would be difficult to over-estimate the weight of this unanimous testimony.
Prayer, salvation brought about in Christ, the action of divine
Providence, are the subjects of hundreds of letters. Some of
my correspondents let it be seen through their letters what
deep intimacy with Christ, what incomparable communion
of souls, can result in marriage from loyalty to these convictions. I will end this account by quoting a typical letter, which
deserves an attentive reading:

'*At this moment my wife and I are sitting opposite each
other at the same table, busy writing. We are intensely happy.
We hardly exchange a word, but we feel so close to one another because we are writing on the same subject, and because we have exactly the same views on this subject. We
know we are completely at one in the love of Christ. My
thoughts are no secret from my wife, just as I have no diffi-*

culty in guessing what she is thinking and feeling at this moment. We know that we, and our children, are journeying together towards our Father's house.

'In my eyes, the wife is for her husband far more than a companion with whom he is called to build his happiness in this world. The journey they have chosen to make together takes them much further than that! By uniting husband and wife in life, as in death, the Lord has made each responsible for the sanctification of the other. As Christ lived for his Church, I try to live for my wife, and to offer up every moment of my life for her. It is my duty to pray for her, but often I pray with her. My constant care is to give her proof of my love, sometimes in words, more often by helping with the housework, by being interested in what she does and by giving her tokens of my trust and faithfulness. Long ago I discovered how much can be done by a word of encouragement, a little admiration, or the countless little attentions with which we can strew our daily path. I try not to be away too often, lest my absence should be the cause of our growing apart or should spoil our intimacy. I try too to be sincere and loyal, kind and understanding. I know that Christ is always at our side. In our home, he is the Friend of the family.'

CREATIVE LOVE

Many letters put the emphasis on this idea: married couples can be completely happy only if their love is creative, as Providence has designed it to be. Nowadays this is a battlefield for very widely differing opinions. It is important for Christians to clarify their ideas on the subject so that they may put them into practice themselves and then spread them among their neighbours.

The community of married people fully achieves reality

when it becomes the source of life. The birth of a first child almost always brings with it a wonderful transformation in the parents' hearts, and the loss of this happiness is the saddest of afflictions for any home. Married couples who yearn for a child and yet are deprived of the joys of parenthood must command all our respect: the home that can never shelter a cradle can be very cold and lonely. And yet even for the childless there is still hope, and the austere vocation to spiritual fruitfulness. Society and the Church owe a vast debt of gratitude to innumerable childless and immeasurably dedicated homes where married couples who can never hold their own child in their arms lavish a parent's love on other people's children.

Married people for whom physical fecundity is possible will come to full self-realisation only if they freely take upon themselves the mission God has entrusted to them. We must be careful here not to undervalue its objective. The vocation of married people requires generosity and warmheartedness. Called to collaborate with God in the work of creation and grace, they must prove their boldness and vitality.

In our society today, unfortunately, a child is so often treated as an intruder. How many of our contemporaries scoff at the mission of married couples in the service of life! Instead of the joys and sorrows of parenthood, they want an easy life of luxury, material pleasures and comfort. Gradually the vocabulary of officialdom has made us familiar with expressions such as 'dependent children'. But, thank God, innumerable homes bear witness to the falsity of this official outlook —homes where each birth is welcomed joyfully, as a blessing that enriches the family. To be happy, a couple must fall in with the wishes of Nature who constantly urges generosity and fecundity. Love is essentially creative. 'Increase and multiply, and fill the earth.' That was the mission God entrusted to men on the day of their creation. And here I speak to young married people first of all, to the new homes in the great family of our diocese. Scores of parents have asked me to stress with all the authority of my office what I am going to tell you now. But I shall not do it in my own words. This is what a well-known gynaecologist writes:

'I have a word of advice for young married people, and that is: Don't wait to have a child until you have bought your house or furnished it as you would like. Take your time over solving these material questions. I myself began my career in a rented house, and my first means of transport was a bicycle. You must know the dangers that threaten your young love and the happiness of your home. Don't delay to set the seal on your love and bring it to full completion in the person of your child. Your young household needs the presence of a little child. Your baby will be a living bond between the parents, who have to withstand the influence of a topsy-turvy world every day of their lives. The baby, frail and weak as he is, will give his parents strength and help them to keep faith with one another.'

I am sure that thousands of married people, with all their experience of life, will subscribe to this testimony. God grant that all may hear it!

The number of children a home can accept from God obviously depends on the health of the parents and the possibilities of education that the household can command. How many children should one have? That is a question for the individual conscience. It is the duty of married people to examine the problem before God. Only they know all the facts. On what grounds can one accuse a couple with few children of pusillanimity? Christ said: 'Judge not, that you may not be judged.' One God has full knowledge of all the family circumstances. Only he knows the motives determining the parents' attitude to the problem of fecundity. Only the supreme Master has the right to judge.

I will not dwell on particular cases here, but I should like to say a word to married couples in general. I should like to tell them: Don't be afraid of a baby—prove your warmth of heart. I say this in the name of thousands of mothers and fathers, who speak from experience; and in the name too of many young people who are disgusted by the selfishness and materialism of so many married couples. I say it in the name of God himself, Father of all wisdom. Be generous! The strength of the bonds uniting you, the security of your love, your happiness in each other and the eternal welfare of your souls urge you not to measure the possibilities too minutely. A certain degree of daring is required in the service of life. Further, you must let yourselves be guided by the thought of all the good you bring into being in the little children to whom you give the inestimable gift of life and union with the love of the Father. Think of this and be glad. How many of us, how many deserving members of the great human family, how many priests, religious and missionaries, how many saints in heaven, owe their existence to their earthly mother's courage and their parents' trust in God?

My dear people, don't misunderstand me. I am not telling you not to be sensible, or recommending you to throw prudence to the winds. But I am asking you to be *generous*. Don't be content with the minimum. Behave like dedicated collaborators with God. You won't repent of it, either in this world, or in eternity. Duty and courage are within the grasp of each of us. But I add for your reassurance: not everyone is called upon to found a *very* large family.

Having said that, and without in any way belittling the

esteem and love we owe to our smaller families, I think it my
duty to ask the Christian community to be fairer in its judg-
ments and to give more respect to parents who have accepted
a great number of children from the hands of God.

The mother of nine children writes me a letter which has
evidently been very carefully thought out:

*'We parents of very large families sometimes have the im-
pression that the Church does not want homes to have very
many children. We have sometimes heard people say: "The
Church has never said that families should have many children." But there is a saying that is often in my mind: "rather
ten on your hands than one on your conscience." We know
that this subject calls for a certain flexibility of mind, and a
subtle way of talking. But please, when priests explain the
new trend, let them not forget a word of respect and encouragement for very big families; life is made very hard for
them. They need the public approval of Holy Church just
as much as they need bread. We are not really unfortunate
or wretched, and we don't want to be treated as though we
were! All things considered, we have the greatest share of
happiness, and we know most joy. We have nine children.
You will realise that this means plenty of work! But we are
fully repaid by the love and affection our children give us in
return. There are so many of them, and their love is so warm-
hearted! And in this immense love we forget all our troubles.
We draw strength from faith and prayer. The thought of
God is with us all day long. Our hearts overflow with gratitude for so much happiness.'*

It is you I am talking to, fathers and mothers of our very
large families. You have given life to so many children, but
not through ignorance, scruple or stupidity, as you are constantly accused of doing. What then was your motive? I make

a point of declaring it in public: your motive, duly deliberated, has been nothing other than love. Fully aware of what you were doing, you determined to devote your vital forces unreservedly to the service of love of your child and of God. Such open-hearted and heroic love commands all our respect. As your bishop and God's representative among you, I pay my homage to you and express my admiration for your warm-hearted love. Why don't people leave you alone? You are doing no harm. Why should you be the only ones not to do as you like? Why are people so intolerant of you, and so aggressive? I don't know. Or does the prophecy of the divine Master apply here: 'If they have persecuted me, they will also persecute you.'? Like Jesus you are mocked, morally scourged and crowned with thorns. But I find a recurrent theme in your letters:

'Father, forgive them, for they know not what they do. If only all these people knew the inexpressible happiness that our heavenly Father pours out upon us! For he repays us unwearingly, a hundred-fold, for all our trouble.'

Be of good cheer, dear and admirable parents! All your life is a glorification of God himself. You will not lack your reward and your crown, for God has said: 'Give, and it shall be given to you; good measure and pressed down and shaken together and running over shall they give into your bosom.' God's generosity is second to none!

Another indispensable condition of lasting love between husband and wife is that they try to show each other their affection. It is not enough that they love; they must make their love clear to one another.

A psychiatrist writes:

'After having been consulted by hundreds of married

people, I am convinced that most failures in marriage are due to lack of mutual understanding. Husband and wife don't talk to each other enough. They are not spontaneous enough in showing what they feel. Sometimes I hear the husband's side, sometimes the wife's, and I so often come to the conclusion that they are attributing to each other intentions which in fact never crossed their mind. If only they could be franker, sincerer, kinder to each other!'

Married couples should realise that the human personality is surrounded by mystery. Every person is a distinct consciousness, and an entirely individual entity. Everyone has direct knowledge of himself, but no creature has immediate access to the emotions of another. God alone fathoms the depths of the heart. Men can arrive at a knowledge of what is in another's consciousness only by means of tangible signs. A word, a handclasp, a smile, a kiss, are outward manifestations of what is going on in the mind. Is it surprising, then, that the community of marriage causes suffering and profound disappointment if husband and wife don't talk enough to each other, or fail to imprint their affection in the natural indications of love?

A wife writes:

'Another disappointing characteristic of my husband—and one to be found in so many others too—is that he is so uncommunicative. He is silent and reserved. And I, who am a woman and sensitive, feel I am useless and superfluous. I sink deeper and deeper into discouragement. In the end this inferiority complex will make me incapable of the slightest effort.'

This is what a priest who often takes retreats for married people always tells them on the first evening:

'My friends, make this retreat into a second honeymoon. Take each other's arm and go off to the other end of the garden. Remember the freshness of your love when you were just married and were so interested in each other, and so attentive, when you had no secrets from each other and tried to translate all your tenderness into loving words and kisses. Yes, make this retreat a new start.'

This is advice that could well be given to all married people. We ought to tell them: Begin your rejuvenation today. Why not confide to each other, as you once did, the feelings that stir the depths of your heart? Be kind and considerate, as you were when you were engaged, when everything promised so well. But the husband will be capable of this subtlety of feeling only if he has learnt to understand feminine psychology and to divine his wife's desires and aspirations, and if he has acquired the knowledge that is the foundation of married life: the art of treating his wife as a woman. And his wife likewise must make the effort to understand her husband's character and mentality, and help him to keep his courage and confidence in all the difficulties of life. No young man or woman should embark on marriage without first undergoing a course of instruction for engaged couples, given by married people.

Many letters stress that courses of lectures on marriage should be arranged here and there in the diocese for engaged couples, where each would have the chance to acquire a better understanding of the other's psychology and obligations. Such courses are already given at some centres, but it is hoped that by next year they will be organised in every deanery. At these centres engaged and newly married couples will have an opportunity to meet married men and women ready to share with them the fruits of their experience of family life.

Please God that all educationists and all families may give
this venture the support it deserves.

When each partner understands the other better, married
couples learn to appreciate more keenly the joy that may lie
in a frank conversation or the simple, spontaneous talks that
are so immensely profitable for their life in common. Here is
a mother of four, writing from the deanery of Roulers, who
has experienced this:

*'There are moments in our family life when we can talk
together seriously and frankly. Often it is after a talk on the
wireless (we have not yet got television), a sermon or a lec-
ture. These conversations are never artificial or thought out
beforehand; it all comes naturally, when the atmosphere is
right . . . and we feel so much better for it! Then we can see
how closely our inmost feelings agree, and how hard we are
each trying, in our particular sphere, to let our children grow
up into fundamentally good people.'*

After twenty-four years of marriage, a doctor and his wife
write as follows:

*'We make every wedding anniversary the time for self-
examination. We ask ourselves if we have been frank and
sincere enough, and kind enough, to one another. We begin
each year as if it were the first. And we can say of ourselves
that after twenty-four years of marriage our love is fonder
and more sensitive than on the first day of our union. And we
believe that all our children, young or grown-up, find a lesson
for their own lives in the proofs of love we give each other.'*

There are many homes in our diocese where there is much
suffering, borne in silence, because married people have not
succeeded in letting their partner see through to their affection and giving proof of their love. So I hope you may learn

to talk simply and quietly to each other. Say what is in your mind. Talk about your joys and sorrows, your daily worries and your ordinary occupations. Everything is interesting to love. All who practise this art of living will agree with the father who writes from the district of La Lys:

'*I would infinitely rather have a peaceful hour with the family than anything television can offer. It is so pleasant to talk over the events of the day, or listen to the children and take an interest in their life at school. That is the programme I would choose for myself, and it is the best there is! My advice is: find time to chat together, parents and children, and talk over the events of the day, great and small.*'

3

The Meeting of
Man and Woman

Two human beings, two Christians, come together in a
lifelong union, and in the sacrament that binds them they
become for each other, in Christ and in his Church, the
source of delight, grace and happiness. How did they meet?
We have touched rapidly on this earlier in this book, but we
must now tackle in more detail the delicate question of the
intimate relations between man and woman.

THE ENGAGEMENT

Many correspondents say unhesitatingly that the happiness
of a married couple depends not only on the choice of a partner but also on the give and take, even in the early stages of
the engagement, between those who have made choice of each
other.

What then should we think about preparation for marriage? Many young people are concerned with this problem
and have written to tell me what they think.

I will summarise here a twenty page essay sent me by a
nineteen-year-old sixth-form boy. It echoes the seriousness
and clear-sightedness which some young people today are

bringing to the problem of marriage. This paper is headed:
'*Engagement: the immediate preparation for marriage.*'

'*There is every indication,' writes this student, 'that not all young people are ready for their initiation into this capacity for happiness at the same moment. Some are quicker than others to achieve the balance they need to stand up to the hazards of life and their emotional troubles. It is generally considered that a young man must be 25 before he has the maturity needed for setting up a home. Girls give the impression of being less stable, but they are in fact usually more mature. Their mental and spiritual development is quicker, perhaps because it reaches its limits sooner.*

'*The engagement is a time of preparation for marriage, but there must also be preparation for engagement. It is common knowledge that many homes split up because the married couple did not have adequate preparation.*'

The choice

The difficulty is to combine obedience with the natural attraction that is indispensable, and with serious reflexion. We are dealing here with a relationship involving all aspects of the human creature, from the most hidden to those most clearly seen and felt. Are adolescents possessed of the criteria they need to practise this important and delicate human art?

According to our young student, these are the conditions of a good choice:

'*First of all* social standing. *To avoid difficulties, it is generally advisable to choose someone with the same social background. This advice may seem commonplace, even humiliating for love; but experience shows how many troubles and difficulties can arise when partners are of entirely different social circumstances.*

'Another point to consider is the degree of culture *of the partner. For instance, an intellectual is not well advised to choose a girl with little education (and the reverse is also true). If the intellectual gap between them is too wide, their centres of interest will be too far apart, and that is the beginning of distortion.*

'It is also important, obviously, to think about character *and aptitudes. Husband and wife must complement one another, if their union is to be stable, lasting and rewarding. Someone who is hopelessly unmethodical and unpunctual doesn't seem the right person to marry a model of tidiness and punctuality. And it is difficult for anyone who sees life through rose-coloured spectacles to live happily with a partner who always has the blues and sees the gloomy side of things.*

'Finally, religious convictions *are of fundamental importance in the choice of partner. In principle, what must be avoided at all costs is an engagement between people of different faiths. Further, it is essential to know exactly how far the religious convictions of the other partner go, and how he intends to bring his religion into his life.'*

'Keeping company'

This is a ticklish problem. What ought our attitude to be during engagement? asks this correspondent. We haven't to look far to see that engagements often end in an impasse. This time in our lives when the best in us should be coming to full flower is unfortunately for many young people only an opportunity to play a game that is superficial, sentimental, and often dangerous. And yet it is during their engagement that a couple should take their bearings for their future

life, and begin to work out the *values* of their home. Mis-
managed engagements are in far too many cases responsible
for the failure of the home.

I must stress an important point here: the respect, the
charity in the noblest and highest sense of the word, that each
of us owes specially to the person he has chosen from among
all others to love him and devote her life to him. For example,
when a young man goes rather too far in a flirtation, he should
realise that he is stealing from the being whom he pretends to
love and admire something of her fairest and loveliest possession. Observers of human psychology believe that for young
people to realise this fundamental and glaring contradiction
is the best way to keep them, throughout the extremely test-
ing time of their engagement, within the bounds of a truly
loving freedom.

'*Where is it best for young engaged people to meet? The
answer is simple enough: in each other's homes. During their
engagement, the young couple get to know each other as
they are, to see each other in all lights, to recognise all the
subtle differences in heart and mind. The deepest and most
delicate qualities of a human being are most easily discerned
in his natural surroundings. How can one possibly get to
know anyone in a cinema, a dance-hall, a fun-fair, or a garden-
party? Married people live their lives in the home, and
preparation for marriage should go on within the family. The
relationships between the girl or the young man and their
people should be carefully observed, for they are very reveal-
ing.*

'*But it is very important too for the engaged couple to
have the chance of serious talks together sometimes, to
confide their tastes and ambitions to each other, to tell each
other again and again, in different ways, how much they love*

each other. Their engagement is something more than a time for tender caresses and sweet words! It is the opportunity to prepare seriously and rationally for life together.

'What should you talk about? Let your fiancée see your special characteristics shining through your tender conversations together. Talk to her about what you find absorbing or interesting. Tell her what place God has in your life, the ideals you are striving for, what you mean to be the measure of your existence. I think it is essential too that engaged couples discuss frankly what their attitude will be to the problem of fecundity. So often the home founders on this reef.'

The rôle of parents and priests

Let us hear what our young correspondent says about this:

'The engaged couple should know that they are not alone at this turning-point in their lives. Their parents are behind them; and their priest too can give them sound advice.

'Parents should help their child in the choice of a companion for life, and the children should be able to confide in them and listen to their advice. The difficulty of the choice comes from its very importance, from the emotional atmosphere which usually surrounds it, not to mention the common reluctance of young people to draw on the experience of their elders. The parents should intervene tactfully and cautiously. They can be sure that head-on opposition to a girl or boy in love will only increase their attachment and make them dig their heels in. And they must always be careful to observe a sensible order of priorities in the criteria of choice. Material questions cannot be completely ignored—at least for people

*who are not very well off—but should never be allowed to
decide the issue.*

*'And parents, though they should exercise some tactful
supervision and avoid dangerous situations, must always respect the personality and the liberty of their children.'*

* * *

*'What part should the priest play here? First of all, he must
focus the young people's attention on the spiritual dimension
of what they are undertaking. He must speak plainly, encourage them to persevere in their love, and not be afraid,
if need be, to point out failings or mistakes; and when at last
the young couple call on him to arrange their wedding, he
should not confine himself to explaining what the ceremony
will cost (and that still happens, unfortunately, in many
parishes), but put forward some ideas to be thought over in
the last weeks of preparation. A priest with any tact will
realise if serious ignorance makes it necessary for him to in-
struct the young man in what he ought to know.*

*'The time of engagement is a time of very great importance.
It will have lasting repercussions on the development of the
couple. Everyone must shoulder his responsibilities here, and
in the first place the engaged couple. After all, it is for them
to decide how they are going to arrange their lives.' And our
correspondent ends his eloquent letter: 'In these very important circumstances a fervent life of prayer will certainly
be an unfailing and most valuable help to them.'*

* * *

It is clear from a great number of letters that this is not
an isolated way of looking at preparation for marriage. This

extract from the joint letter of a score of technical students, aged between 17 and 19, gives fresh evidence of this:

'*The initiation of young people should not be left too late. Many have ruined their marriages even before their wedding day, and very often through ignorance. Then they say: "If only we had known!" What ought they to know and do? Simply to learn to love—they court each other without really getting to know each other—to practise self-giving; to ask advice, if need be, from a doctor or priest, so as to check up on their own opinions. We would also add an S.O.S.: don't leave young people to learn about life in the army or the factory. Can anything be done to avoid that?*'

* * *

What is the girl's attitude to marriage nowadays? It is obvious that many young women embark on marriage in a thoroughly thoughtless and childish way. But those who think seriously about the future show a certain uneasiness going hand in hand with a great deal of idealism. The two letters which follow are characteristic of this state of mind.

A girl student of 19 writes:

'*If I am quite honest with myself, I must admit that I know only very few really happy homes. Most of them seem happy, but when you look more closely you see that this is not always the case. That is why I am really afraid to plunge into life. We are still at school, and supposed not to have any worries yet. But I must confess that sometimes I do worry about what will happen to me. The happiness of a family sometimes depends on a mere trifle: a little more kindness or mutual understanding. But we should have the courage to face these realities. I am quite convinced, it is true, that to a large extent it rests with me whether my marriage "works", but still I am worried about it. In the few really happy homes I know, happiness does not, I think, spring from chance, temperament, accommodation, or a large income. The roots of happiness go deeper. And love comes in here, mutual understanding, patience, willingness to forget oneself for one's partner and the children, self-abnegation and self-giving.*

'*Unfortunately that sort of happiness is very rare. I am sure that strength for it comes only from prayer, the life of God within us.*'

'*Now that I am 18,*' writes another girl, '*I expect a great deal of my future husband and the father of my children. I think it is extremely important for married people to tell each other frankly, honestly and spontaneously about their mutual difficulties, the problems of house and children. That is why I think an understanding, mutual love is essential. For married people to be able to accept the inevitable difficulties and troubles and weather them together, I am sure that what is needed is prayer together, in which the children should join as soon as they are old enough, and a deep sacramental life.*

'*I want too for us to live our married life really together, not just to be him at work and me at home. So I don't think I am unreasonable in wanting him to come home after work and then really be "at home", not to come back only wanting to eat, read his paper or watch television and then go to bed, but to stay and talk about his work with me and take an interest in what I do. This may seem rather sentimental, but all the same I should like him to show me little attentions now and then, give me a helping hand and sometimes let me see how warmly he loves me. When I am a mother, I shall want my husband to be a good and truly loving father to our children, taking an affectionate interest in them and their education. It should be a normal thing for father and mother to discuss difficulties with their children, and help and advise them. Why should that be left to the mother?*

'I think that if a husband lives for his home like this, there is a very good chance that the home will stay united!'

INTIMACY IN MARRIAGE

Some married people have lived side by side for years without ever achieving that deep union to which they are called in virtue of their marriage. The grace of the Lord can make this communion in marriage so intimate and so complete that it is like the indescribably deep and close union in love of Jesus Christ and his spiritual bride, the One, Holy, Catholic and Apostolic Church. Why is communion in marriage so rarely achieved? The reason lies partly in certain factors on the human plane; the husband or wife, sometimes both, lack the necessary degree of savoir-faire, experience or courage. And also, the married couple may not let themselves be guided in their life together by the principles of the Christian faith, the source of so much joy and courage.

The rôle of the husband

What follows now is a 'joint' letter. After consulting his wife, a husband writes to me about his long experience of home life; they have belonged for some years to a society for the encouragement of spiritual life in the home.

'First of all we should like to thank you for taking the initiative in consulting the Christians of your diocese on the problems of Christian families and homes. We cannot disregard an appeal that comes from Christ's representative among us. This then is the small stone we can contribute to the building as a whole.

'*We have been told of the problem of some wives who complain of their husbands' clumsiness in marital relations. My wife and I have decided to be as honest as we can on this subject, delicate though it is. We hope that these notes may be of help to some of our brethren in marriage.*

'*The problem of physical relations between husband and wife is one of the greatest importance. This is proved by the spate of books and pamphlets on the subject in the last few years. But when we compare some of these publications with our own experience, we are uneasy about their approach to the problem.*

'*Let us admit from the start that the object of getting married is to bring about as perfect a union as possible. That being so, what place does "sex" play in the success (not to say the happiness) of the union of husband and wife?*

'*To begin with, here are some notes based on our own experience, which may then serve as a basis for our conclusions.*

'*1. "Sexual" is not simply the same thing as "physical". From one point of view everything that characterises a man in his relations with a woman, and vice versa, can be called sexual; but it cannot be denied that there is also a sexuality of feeling, of the mind and soul. And so any attempt to make physical sexuality alone the basis of harmony in marriage is very mistaken.*

'*2. The different spheres of sex—physical, emotional, intellectual and spiritual—are closely bound up together. And we have come to the conclusion that there can be no true physical union unless at the same time there is union of hearts, minds and souls. The converse is equally true.*

'*Here is where the drama often lies: in the fact that each of a man's energies is bent on satisfying self alone. Often one partner—usually the husband—is looking for no more*

3*

in physical union than the satisfaction of his physical needs, and treats the other just as the object of sensual enjoyment. This is a very serious error, and springs from the anarchy within man that is the result of original sin. It not only inflicts deep wounds on the other partner, but leaves the guilty one unsatisfied. Such unions excite sensuality without appeasing it and, still worse, create a state of tension between husband and wife, and an almost physical revulsion. We believe that this commonly leads to divorce. To sum up, physical union is valid only if it is the expression of complete love between husband and wife.

'But there is more to it than that: physical union is the expression of love, and at the same time its food. Though physical union inspired by selfish passion produces a feeling of repugnance and helps to separate husband and wife, yet it can bring them complete satisfaction and an atmosphere of kindness and love when it transcends itself in a true communion of heart and mind.

'It would hardly be an exaggeration to say that a husband can come together with his wife even when his mind is engaged in solving a geometry theorem. A woman's reaction, on the other hand, is all of a piece, and involves her whole being. Some people think she is more "unified" and therefore more human than a man. But this is arguable, for every organic unit includes clearly distinct elements. At all events, the fact remains, and the husband should bear it in mind. The "complementariness" of man and woman is confirmed at every level, and particularly the physical.

'The initiative must come from the man; the relative passivity of his wife is not without spiritual and moral significance: all through her married life, the woman makes use of her special innate gifts and wins the mysterious victories of femininity in a kind of general submissiveness. But it is a ridi-

culous exaggeration to represent the man's sexuality simply as possession, the woman's as oblation. Both, if we look deep enough, are self-giving, but each in a different form.

'The initiative is left to the husband not for his own personal satisfaction, but because it answers to his temperament, and above all because that is the wish of the woman. He exercises this "direction" in sympathy with his wife's needs, temperament and desires.

'St Paul's words are not out of place here: "Husbands, love your wives as your own bodies." In other words, "Show your wife the same respect and attentions as you would show your other self." And to do that the husband must learn to know that other self, and to adapt his attitude and actions to the needs of his wife. It is distressing to have to say: "Of all things on earth, a man knows least about a woman." And the converse is also true, even if to a lesser degree.

'Physical union is thus by no means the red light for instinct; it is discipline, self-forgetfulness, testimony, love.

'3. The union of bodies is willed by God, since it is written into nature. It is a wonderful thing, if it is accomplished according to God's design, that is as both the expression and the means of love in marriage. Parenthetically, we feel it is more important to stress this aspect of God's will than to invoke a narrow ethical code of what is "allowed" and "not allowed".

'And now let us try to draw our conclusions:

'(a)   The human being is one, and physical union cannot be treated as an end in itself, or dissociated from all the other aspects of life in common. In fact, it is written into the nature of married life. We are sure that in a home where there is no atmosphere of understanding, the physical union of husband and wife can only result in disappointment.

'So we must condemn the attitude that strives after per-

fection on the physical plane and neglects all the other spheres. That is a form of epicurism doomed to weariness and failure. Only the immense and wonderful variety of the spiritual world can give ever new meaning to the constant repetition of the same gestures and caresses. Relationships based on sex alone are almost always short-lived.

'(b)   Physical union, like the union of husband and wife in general, must have its foundation in self-forgetfulness. It is wrong to think that the only embraces worth anything are the so-called "spontaneous" ones, which are in fact dictated by instinct. Two partners in marriage who come together with the calm, express intention of giving themselves to each other achieve a union often of a far higher order than those that rely more on instinct.

'(c)   Since the initiative is the husband's, the quality of the union depends on him. We would not go so far as to say that the wife has no responsibility in the matter; on the contrary, by the general atmosphere in the home, the care she devotes to her own body, her warm-hearted acceptance of her husband's overtures, and her response to his approach, she too contributes in large measure to the perfect accomplishment of their union. We simply mean that in the immediate present, here and now, the husband straight away sets their physical union in an atmosphere of total love, or else makes it into no more than a series of obscene actions designed to satisfy his own sensuality. We think, then, that with a few exceptions where the wife is really inadequate, failures in this sphere are almost entirely the result of the errors and clumsiness of the husband.

'(d)   Finally, we must put physical union back in its rightful place. God wished it to be not an act of shame, nor the one aim of marriage, but the means by which the love between husband and wife is expressed and developed, and also the

way that leads to the joys of fecundity. Thus, like all acts of love, it proceeds from the love of God, and possesses an eternal value in its own right. We feel that a clearer perception of this value would often be of great benefit to Christian couples, for awareness of it would help them to live their lives better on the physical plane.

'We have tried to put the best of our experience into these reflexions, in as discreet a form as we could, and we hope they will in some measure, however small, help some other Christian homes. Even if this were not to be so, they will certainly have succeeded in helping us at least to a better understanding of the purpose of God in married life. For this reason we are grateful to you for having invited us to share our experience and the fruit of our reflexions with others.'

*   *   *

What should the husband do for his wife's happiness in the intimacy of marriage? It is difficult to suggest a programme of living which would apply to every partner. No two situations are completely parallel, no two temperaments quite identical. We can give general rules of conduct, but these must be adapted to each particular case with discernment and wisdom. And anyone who tries to put them into practice in everyday life needs a good share of courage and perseverance. Discernment and wisdom, courage and perseverance, are natural gifts, but in the soul of baptised Christians they gradually flower under the action of the Holy Spirit. Since man is passionate by nature, and has lost his harmony and balance through original sin, he has to find them again. If he invokes the Holy Spirit regularly, if he tries to follow his divine inspiration, his lost virtues will be born again, will bring order into his life, and gradually recover their spontaneity.

That is why the Christian husband will have a special devotion to the Holy Spirit. And his wife will join in his prayer to
the Breath of God.

The rôle of the wife

In Christian marriage, man and woman have equal rights.
And they have the same duty to strive to 'meet' each other
in the very depths of their being. That presents problems for
the husband and for the wife as well. She too must make an
effort, enhancing all her natural femininity. She too must
face the question: How can I really meet the man the Lord
is leading me to, in the very depths of his individual being?

To help answer this question, I quote here the letter a
young woman received from her mother on her wedding day:

'*This evening you will be alone together for the first time
in your own home, and this will be your first letter—a letter
from Mother, to welcome you there and wish you happiness.*

'*Probably you are sitting very close to each other as you
read this, sometimes looking into each other's eyes—the eyes
in which Daddy and I saw your love spring into life and
growth, the love the Lord has consecrated today, the love
which in all its fullness is now to be your life.*

'*My letter isn't meant to disturb your happiness, but to join
in it and, I hope, to throw more light on it.*

'*Soon you will go up to your bedroom. Daddy and I advised
you to make it as personal, as much "your own", as you
could. This is what we did ourselves, because, in married
life, the bedroom is, as it were, what the altar is in church.
Nothing is good enough, beautiful enough, for it; it is meant
for sacred things.*

'*It is in your bedroom that you will find rest, composure,
the time to be fully yourselves and the time to be each other's.*

When you shut the door you must forget your work, your worries, and the world outside. There is nowhere you can talk together better.

'My dear daughter, make sure that every morning you are as radiant as you are today, as well groomed, as feminine, and as glad to be a woman, to be young, to be given entirely to the man who is your husband before God and men.

'When he comes back tired from work in the evening, let him relax in your arms—your arms that must always be waiting for him so that he shall not look for others. Let him drink his fill of your charms, so that he shall not thirst anywhere else. Let him fall under the spell of your grace and attractiveness, so that no other charms shall allure him more.

'A man is a man, darling. Especially later, when habit begins to rub the gloss off your life together, he must be able to give way to his longing to possess you. It is up to you to keep his longing alive, and to stimulate it.

'A woman, they say, is very ingenious when she is in love. Why should she be less so when it comes to exploring the great and beautiful mystery, which God himself has blessed, of complete unity with her husband?

'You lavish a thousand and one little attentions on him. You are grateful to him for watching over you, working for you, and protecting you. You know his tastes and his little weaknesses. . . . Since this morning, when you gave yourselves to one another in the sacrament of marriage, your husband has acquired rights over you. But don't be passive when the time comes for him to exercise them; he must win his way afresh into the treasure-house every time.

'I know how your thoughts and feelings, your prayers and your work, your heart and your happiness, are all dominated by the man you want in your woman's heart to know your master. But he must be the object of your desires too. Why

not tell him so, why not show him so, in a different way every day? Perhaps some other woman will try to tell him or show him, with no right at all.

'I don't want to make you jealous—of course not! Real love, St Paul says, envieth not; but your husband doesn't live on a desert island, does he?

'You may be sure that there will be times when your figure won't be as lovely as it is today, for instance when, please God, you are expecting a baby, or as you grow older. But you know as well as I do that married love, even in its most intimate moment, does not seek the union of two bodies only, but of two beings, heart, soul and individuality. You as well as I will come to find that what matters most in marriage is not the physical expression of love, but that all the same this is a very, very important factor in it. It is worth making an effort here, even when you are tired or on edge; true love forgets self for the beloved.

'But, darling, never make your husband feel that you regard the gift of yourself as a "sacrifice", part of your duty as a wife. No, make him feel he has to win you, stimulate his urge to conquer and dominate . . . this is what gives most pleasure to a loving wife.

'Why shouldn't your eyes always be as bright as they are today? Don't let them be cold and indifferent when you read the desire in his. Let your eyes allure and tempt him . . . show him that you love to see him, to look at him.

'Why shouldn't your soft, slender hands show him your love? You caress things you admire. Don't you admire him, don't you think he is handsome? All right; let him feel it in the touch of your fingers.

'Why shouldn't you let him see how you rejoice in the warmth of his presence? Never be indifferent to his kisses, *his voice, his caresses. Don't you enjoy his courtship? Then show him that you do, otherwise he might lose his wish to court you; much happiness is destroyed because the wife was not responsive to her husband's invitation to the ever-new game of love.*

'*Show him, dear wife of my new son, and go on showing him. Tell him, go on telling him, gaily or sadly, seriously or jokingly, softly or passionately, that you love him, and only him, that you belong to him alone.*

'*Of course you will sometimes be tempted to begin a flirtation, but be careful, dear daughter, you may burn your fingers! To begin with, you find it flattering—a married woman whom other men are interested in. . . . But a husband can't be expected to behave like a lapdog when he is provoked. And you know what they say: You can't build your happiness on the ruins of another's.*

'*Your song of love must always be for him, today, and later—though you may think this is absurd—when you hold his child in your arms and all your being thrills with love for the baby brought forth by you, conceived by him, blessed by God.*

'*Your husband must always have first place. You are his wife first of all, only after that the mother of his child. Your mutual love had to come first, before you could know maternal love. Never forget that; a mother is not indispensable, as I am finding out for myself now, but a wife is.*

'*That is all I have to say. I don't know if you have understood, dear daughter. Make your husband happy—no, be his happiness.*

'God bless you—that is your mother's prayer.'

*　　*　　*

What we have just written about the meeting of husband and wife in Christian marriage will make sad reading for any partner deserted by the other.

To all who have been through this tribulation I would repeat the words of Jesus: 'Look up and lift up your heads, because your redemption is at hand' (Luke 21; 28).

A forsaken husband writes:

'My wife has left me and the children. My grief knows no bounds. But I forgive her in my heart. If only she knew how much I love her still! If I have done wrong—and who is perfect?—I am sorry from the bottom of my heart. And I still look for her return. Every evening I pray with the children for "our mother", and that she may come back to us. If not, at least I hope that she will ask God's pardon before she dies. Then God will give her back to me, for in his eyes I am her rightful husband. I offer my suffering for her salvation, for our eternal reconciliation in the peace of paradise.'

When the death of one of the partners has interrupted the intimacy of the home, the calvary of life alone begins for the other. And the closer the bond, the harder the separation. It is a deep consolation then to be able to look back on the past with self-respect and a clear conscience, as does the aged widow who writes:

'Yes, I do know one happy home: my own. Now we are separated by death, but I am happy because we had such a beautiful life together; death cannot alter that beauty, and it still lives on. . . .

'This, briefly, was our life: we were married forty years ago. Our marriage was blessed by eight children. We went short of a good many things, for my husband was a working-man who had to cross the frontier into France every day to

*earn the family's bread. But we were as happy as kings with
our fine family.*

'*What gave us the strength for a life like this? Our mutual
love. Everything we did, we did for the other, and we comforted each other in sorrow and in joy. We taught our children
to pray, as our parents had taught us. Prayer is a great support. I am indeed sorry for those who don't know how to
pray in misfortune.*

'*We often said to each other: should we go hungry if we
had one more to feed? No, the more children we had, the
happier we were, and we were none the poorer for it.*

'*The children grew up, and the time came to think of their
future. Each of them was able to choose a trade that suited
his capacity and his inclinations. Today our three daughters
in their turn are wives and mothers. They are good house-
wives, and give their children the upbringing they were given
themselves at home.*

'*Our five sons have learnt a trade, as I said. They earn
their living honestly and bring up their sons as their own
father taught them.*

'*We were so happy. . . . We had our savings, and our pen-
sion meant that we needn't fear the future. We were talking
about it together one evening, saying how happy we were to
have lived like this, and how we hoped to have many more
years of happiness. Scarcely an hour after our evening
prayers and this talk together, my husband died suddenly of
a ruptured artery. Now I am alone, but I am still happy. I go
to church every day to pray for my husband, for my children
that they may know the same happiness. And I pray for myself too, that I may be upheld and comforted in the trial of
separation. The eight families are very happy too, and often
come to see "Mummy". Yes, Monsignor, there are plenty of
happy homes. You don't need to be rich for that. The people*

who have most difficulties are often the best rewarded.
  '*I am a grandmother nineteen times over, and the number*
of grandchildren will go up again this year, please God. I
would not exchange my happiness for anything in the world.
My children are my pride, my honour, and the joy of God
in my life.'

When death puts an end to the union of husband and wife
on earth, they must each appear before the Lord, who is the
Father of mercy but also the supreme Judge. Those who have
lived a good life will be admitted, after they are purified, to
eternal light, to the indescribable and infinite joy of full
friendship with God. Then they will meet the Father they
have known and served as their father, the Son with whom
they have worked in their home and neighbourhood, the Holy
Spirit who was their guide and gave them even on earth a
foretaste of eternal bliss.

Will married people in eternity be united only with God,
or will there be new and perfect union between those who
were husband and wife on earth? After this life, Christian
couples will find each other again in Jesus Christ, just as they
were united in Christ by the sacrament of matrimony. They
will find their children again, unless by living in guilt and
dying in sin these children have voluntarily and for ever
made themselves unworthy of this infinite joy of the family.
In heaven the happiness of the home will be restored, but now
without failings or set-backs, disagreements or misunder-
standings, worries or misgivings, physical needs or passions.

In the supreme activity of eternity, at the very heart of the
Most Holy Trinity, each will be all light, love and unity:
that will be the beginning of perfect and everlasting union.

4

The Meeting of God
and the Home

The unity of the Christian home is a supreme blessing, and under the protection of God. The Father constantly sends his Holy Spirit to the community of the Christian family. Filled with the Spirit of God, husband and wife bind themselves to each other in all the generosity of their love, in the image of Christ's active union with his Church. Every community that brings together men baptised, confirmed and married in religion, is the constant care of divine providence.

In these difficult times especially, the greatest consolation of the family lies in the cheering words of Jesus: 'I say to you, who are my friends: Fear ye not them that kill the body and are not able to kill the soul; but rather fear him that can destroy both soul and body in hell. Are not two sparrows sold for a farthing? And not one of them shall fall on the ground without your Father ... Fear not therefore; better are you than many sparrows ... Be not solicitous for your life, what you shall eat, nor for your body, what you shall put on. Is not the life more than the meat and the body more

85

than the raiment? . . . Consider the lilies of the field, how they grow; they labour not, neither do they spin. But I say to you that not even Solomon in all his glory was arrayed as one of these. And, if the grass of the field, which is today and to-morrow is cast into the oven, God doth so clothe; how much more you, O ye of little faith? . . . Be not solicitous therefore . . . Your Father knoweth that you have need of all these things. Seek ye therefore first the kingdom of God and his justice; and all these things shall be added unto you. Fear not, little flock, for it hath pleased your Father to give you a kingdom.'

Jesus' moving words are an inexhaustible source of consolation for God's little flock, the Christian family. The Shepherd is always beside those who sincerely desire to live by their divine sonship.

The number of married couples who daily meditate on the content of their faith, who seek to deepen it, to live it all the days of their life, is mounting, you may be sure. They are not Catholics simply through heredity or habit; they have gladly accepted the inestimable gift of faith, and gladly make it bear fruit. God is not for them, as he is for some, a kind of insurance, whose favour will protect us from all the ill-fortune and accidents that lie in wait for us. No, for sincere Christians, God is the life of their life. And they know perfectly well that their obedience to God will not give them immunity from trials, illness, and vexations. They do not ask for miracles, and realise that it would ill accord with divine wisdom to be constantly making exception to the ordinary laws of nature. What they seek in the first place is the Kingdom of God. What they desire is the Reign of the Father, and that his Will be done on earth as it is in heaven.

Such married Christians, deep in their hearts, will never be the prey of real troubles. They have faith, faith that at once stimulates and soothes, faith which tells them that they are the 'little flock' that the Good Shepherd watches over, members of God's family, and that the supreme Father has infinite love for his children. And that they are worth more than many sparrows.

They endure their sufferings in union with Christ crucified. They see in them a means of sharing in the sanctification of their home and the salvation of the world. They know that they must carry out a mission of charity, each through the other, that overflows on to their children. If they dedicate themselves wholly to this mission, God will give strength to their mutual love, and kindle in their inmost hearts his joy and happiness. The dimensions of the human heart are limitless. Suffering makes man unhappy, but it is not by acquiring wealth that he becomes truly rich: happiness comes from mutual love. Nothing, nothing in the world can alloy the ineffable felicity of those who know they are deeply and intensely loved, and above all, above all, devote themselves to love, the supreme activity of man. Those who bring their Catholicism superficially into their lives have no idea of the intense happiness which even on earth awaits married couples who, in full awareness of the truths of their faith, understand the deep significance of their sacramental covenant and strive for the increase of divine life within the soul of their partner and their children.

This is what a happy couple writes, after a long life together. As you will see, the action we have taken for the protection of family life has stirred old memories, and they have written to tell me of a life-time's experience.

In their message every married couple can find a programme for their own life.

'We are gradually becoming an old household. How often

*we have heard our grandparents, and even our parents, talk
of the "good old days"! And we sometimes use the phrase
ourselves, though jokingly: all thinking people must realise
that better times are within humanity's reach. . . . You have
only to think of the general increase in comfort and easy
living, the opportunities for education, etc. And yet is it so
unreasonable to praise the past? For ourselves, we believe
that the "old days" were "good" because most people clung
to the real values that the younger generation so mistakenly
despise. And by that we mean: a simple, less restless way of
life, a deep faith in God, a Christian conception of life in
marriage, an unshakeable trust in Divine Providence, and
good neighbourliness founded on mutual kindness and sympathy.*

'*Are these outworn values? We know many homes where
they are still held in honour. In our long life we have got to
know many happy households. In our opinion, the factors
we have listed determine even today the happiness of the
home.*

'PEACE AND CALM. *Experience has shown us how harmful a
restless life is to the happiness of the home. Nothing is more
salutary and refreshing after a worrying day than to come
back to the peace and intimacy of the home.*

'FAITH IN GOD. *Trust in Divine Providence helps the home to
surrender itself not to blind fate, but to the love of God who
is our Father and orders all things for our eternal happiness,
which is prefigured by peace and happiness in this world.*

'A CHRISTIAN LIFE IN MARRIAGE. *This supposes complete
trust in the partner, and excludes any unnatural practices,
which are always prejudicial to our spiritual and nervous
equilibrium. In such a life the deep joys of parenthood are
compensation enough for the cares and anxieties that inevitably beset a father or mother. The partners in marriage*

lift each other towards God, the Master of life. Their com-munity, even in its deepest physical expression, becomes a source of satisfaction. It leads them to better knowledge and appreciation of each other's character and psychology, better understanding of how partners in a marriage, each with his own qualities and failings, complete and perfect each other. A Christian life in marriage will help husband and wife to bring their love to full flower and to strengthen their spiritual and religious foundations, especially at times of enforced con-tinence.

'GOOD NEIGHBOURLINESS. *A local community pervaded by a Christian spirit is charity's forcing-house. It provides count-less opportunities for helping and being helped; and surely it is this that best shows the truth of the saying: "It is a more blessed time to give, than to receive."*

'*Such a conception of life can be summed up in the three great acts: the act of faith in God, the act of hope in him who is our Father and governor of the world, the act of charity towards God and our neighbour.*

'*Is this kind of life within our reach? Our long experience has brought us into contact with many families who have put it into practice. But if they are to conform with that ideal, Christian couples must find the strength they need in prayer and the life of the sacraments. There they come into contact with God, their Father. As far as they can, they bring him into all their actions and behaviour. With him they journey through this world to the life to come, strengthened and up-held by the certainty that God himself is in the end the happi-ness for which they have been created. Near him and in him they hope to meet again one day, with their children, for all eternity. He is their strength, their hope and their love.*'

Without prayer, the home can never become the high place

of love. Prayer is the essential condition if members of a family are to live deeply attached to one another and achieve the unity of heart and mind that springs from grace in those who are ready to seek first the Kingdom of God. Prayer alone can create mutual trust, prayer alone helps us to share every joy and sorrow. Such union is a gift from God, and married couples must ask it of the Father in all simplicity, through the intercession of Christ in whom their union was sealed.

'This is a question that is bound to occur to one sometimes,' writes a young couple: 'how did this stranger become my husband, how did this unknown girl become my wife? Was it just chance? In everything that happens to us, should we not see the hand of God? Is it not God who united us as man and wife at the altar, and has ratified our union once and for all? If God is really at the beginning of our adventure, he will not fail to guide us on our path and to help us, if only we will ask him not so much to clear the obstacles from our path, as to help us to surmount them.'

This touching letter comes from a mother:

'Sunday mass is never too long for me; it is my week-end rendezvous with the Lord. I commit everything to him, joys and sorrows. At the consecration, I always say: "Lord, make your infinite love the bulwark that keeps us all together. Make our children loyal Christians and true apostles."—Our lives are in his hand. My husband and I have hearts overflowing with gratitude for the happiness he grants us. We have got to know a family which does not believe in God. Each of them lives for himself. The children do just as they like. A home like that is a hell! Our children sometimes compare the two homes, and they always come to the same conclusion: "It is

much better in our house, we are really happy. Daddy and mummy are strict, but that's because it is good for us."

'Monsignor, you are the shepherd of our souls; pray for us, that every home and every human being may know the happiness we know!'

It is very important that young married people should start praying together *their first evening.* Now that they are embarking on life together, they must stop thinking what other people will say, and pray together very simply every evening, give each other the blessing and ask the All Highest and his divine Mother to be beside them and help them in the task which is now to direct their whole life. From that day on, they can say the act of charity together, being careful to mention each other: 'My Lord and God, I love thee above all things, with all my heart, with all my strength, because thou art infinitely perfect and to be loved above all things, and I love my neighbour, especially my dearest wife, my dearest husband, as myself, for love of thee. In this love I would live and die.'

'From the first day of our marriage, we have always added after our evening prayers (a decade of the Rosary and a blessing exchanged between us), once we are in bed, a second decade that the Lord will help us to safeguard our happiness and never to do anything that could in any way prejudice the integrity of our married life. In our home there is plenty of work to be done, and every day brings its share of cares and worries. But we are deeply happy. Thank God, we are all in good health, and what is more important, we know we can fully count on each other. We owe this happiness and knowledge, I am sure, to him who watches over us from heaven and to our heavenly Mother, for whom I have always had a particular devotion. At Lourdes we entrusted our future*

*and our marriage to our Mother's care, I as a girl in 1949,
and then both of us as a newly married couple in 1955. It
is in her we have found the strength and conviction which
are the mainstay of our life.'*

As mutual love grows, intimacy with the Lord will grow
in like measure. Gradually husband and wife will learn to live
together in God's sight, knowing always that Jesus Christ
is at their side to help and guide them in their love. He is
the living bond, the way, the truth and the life. In suffering
he is consolation; in weakness and sin, he is pity and
healing.

*'In times of trouble,' writes a husband, 'it is more salutary
to call on the Holy Virgin, the source of purity, than to brood
over our faults and failings. It is not enough to be on our
guard against particular and ever more subtle forms of evil:
we must above all pray God for grace, through the merits
of Jesus Christ, for only grace and prayer can rescue us from
the slough of sin.'*

*'Our marriage is perfectly united and happy,' writes a
household in another diocese. 'In our happiness we see not
the result of chance but an undeserved gift from God, for
which we thank him daily from the bottom of our hearts.
We are self-employed. Our income fluctuates and our house
is old and inconvenient. We are often hard put to it to make
both ends meet, and it is out of the question for us to buy
everything we should like. But we are profoundly happy, and
our happiness increases with each child we have. We attribute
our happiness to the fact that we live for one another. Our
constant concern is to make each other happy. From the very
beginning we decided to live very simply, and to banish luxury
and vanity from our home. We try to be honest and sincere*

with each other. We love each other as we are, and put up good-humouredly with what we like less. There is another important factor: we have never used any methods of birth control. I feed the babies myself for as long as possible, and so we have managed to keep births reasonably spaced out. We both love children and hope to have a very big family. We have been married for nearly 11 years and are expecting our seventh child. The Lord took our fifth to himself. We hardly ever go out, and find our happiness at home.

'And now this is the most important thing of all: we have complete trust in God and a great love for the Virgin. We recite the rosary every day, and receive the sacraments as often as we can, with our children. We are infinitely grateful to God for our upbringing, and the Christian faith which is the source of our love.'

Here is another letter, signed 'Just a Mother':

'I can say in all sincerity that I am very happy in my home life. And yet I have not been spared tribulation. At the beginning of our marriage a serious failing in my husband caused me great suffering. Every morning, without fail, I finished my prayers with an Ave for him. I persevered and my prayer was heard. After long years of patience and trust in God, my husband has become a good Christian, fervent and sincere. We understand each other very well now. I find great satisfaction in my children too. I go to church every morning, and am sure I am setting them a good example. When any misunderstanding casts a gloom on our home I make a great effort, sometimes at considerable cost to myself, for after all I am as sinful as anyone else. I try to smooth out difficulties with a smile and a pleasant word. In the course of the day I often find myself singing. I feel that a mother who can sing is a mother who can get through her difficult task of bring-

ing up the children every day, and so contribute to the glory of God in this world and the welfare of her home. No, it isn't comfort or a large income that make for happiness. My house is only small, and I have to work miracles to make both ends meet. And yet I can say truly that I wouldn't for anything in the world exchange my lot with all the ladies I see driving round in their big American cars. For me, and I speak from experience, happiness lies in a deeply Christian life. It consists of accepting from God whatever each day brings, joys or sorrows. We must have boundless trust in God, for he is truly the best of fathers and watches jealously over all his children; he will never forsake any of them. The Holy Virgin too has an important place in my life; she is the mother of us all, and we should look in vain for an earthly mother so sensitive. No, nothing can give us such deep peace and happiness as a truly Christian life. That alone can help us to put up with the faults of others, for who is without fault? The mother is the mainstay of the home: in her it is either built up or broken up.'

And the next letter brings out clearly what the love of Christ can accomplish in the heart of a wife. The young woman who writes it had great disappointments to contend with at the beginning of her marriage. Her husband's goodness and generosity then touched her deeply.

'One day when I was coming back from work I felt the need to pour out my heart to the Lord. I went into church for the evening Mass. What a blessing it was to be able to talk with him, to confide all my worries and desires to him! I had lived so long as if he didn't exist! This meeting with him made a far deeper impression on me than anyone could have foreseen. Christ came visibly into my life. He literally

took possession of me, and I prayed: "Lord, whatever your plans for me, I am ready to sacrifice everything to fall in with them. Thy will be done, not mine. Help me to be responsive to the slightest sign of your love." To become a mother, to give life to a child, suddenly seemed to me a vocation so sublime that it made me tremble, and inwardly I began to desire it with my whole heart. I prayed about it and asked the Lord for grace to receive life and carry it within me, that he might use it later. The impression these moments of intense recollection made on me has never faded. Every day I thank him again and pray: "Lord, make me a holy mother, an obedient tool in thy hands, a messenger of grace and benediction."

'*At night, when I come back utterly exhausted by my work and the long journey, I go into my parish church as I pass, so great is my hunger for the Lord and so much do I feel that he is my strength. And I pray: "Jesus, I am very tired, but I accept it for love of you. Bless my husband, bless our home. Bless us. We must do great things for you, who deign to use our help in building the world."*

'*Next day, when I go off at dawn, I renew my offering of the day, thinking of all the men and women who are with me in the bus, and I pray that the Lord may grow in their lives too, in the factory or office and in the neighbourhood where they live. And my burning desire is that they too may one day know what it is to possess the Lord.*'

Christian couples will gradually learn to talk with Jesus of everything that concerns their home. In his work the husband will remember the Lord and stop for a moment to say a brief prayer for his family; so too will the wife left at home alone or with small children. In Christ her thoughts will find her husband working away from home. And each knows the other is talking to the Lord, so that Christ becomes for them a living means of contact, which allows them to be still united through all their preoccupations and in spite of distance.

'We embarked on life with nothing but true love and boundless confidence in divine providence. We have lived through some very dark hours, and yet, after twenty years of marriage, we begin each day with the sign of the cross, a short act of thanksgiving for the night's rest, and the offering of all our actions. Throughout the day I often find God again; I thank him for my happiness and when doubts or worries assail me I take refuge in him. Every evening after dinner, which my husband's profession makes it easy for us to have all together, we say our evening prayers, adding a decade of the Rosary for all priests and vocations.'

Love of Christ and generous service devoted to him may inspire and direct a whole life-time, from extreme youth to old age. The letter of a mother, now elderly, is proof of this:

'At school they told us of the Jewish custom for mothers to offer the first fruits of their love in thanksgiving, and dedicate them to God. I resolved then that if I got married and was expecting a child, I would offer this first fruit of our union to the Lord.

'After our marriage, when I knew I was pregnant, I told my husband what I intended. As he was a sincere Christian I had no difficulty in getting his consent. From that moment we both prayed that the Lord would accept our offering.

'After the birth of our first son our union was blessed five times more by the arrival of a baby. Each time we offered it to the Lord.

'Of course we have never breathed a word of this to the children; it is the parents' duty to leave them completely free.

'*God was gracious and accepted our first offering; our eldest son became a priest. Later on two of our daughters entered the convent. What have we done to deserve such happiness?*

'*I am a widow now, but in the evening of my life I renew the offering I made in my youth: every day I ask the Lord to accept the fruits of my motherhood.*'

HOW THE CHILDREN MEET THE LORD

It is said that it is for the mother to show her children the way that leads to the heart of God. That is perfectly true. But they are doubly blessed if their father too guides them on this path. So it is very important to consider the means that parents should use in this supreme task of religious education.

On Good Friday this year I received this letter from a doctor's wife:

'*I should like to send you a few lines on the importance of prayer in our family. We so often feel ourselves profoundly at one, thanks to the prayers we say together.*

'*On the way to school, I pray with my younger son: "Lord Jesus, I offer thee today, little as it is, all I am and have in this world."*

'*On Sunday when we are out in the car conversation sometimes stops for a moment, as we pass a roadside cross or a chapel, so that we can say a Hail Mary.*

'*At midday we say grace before lunch. This always creates a favourable impression, even when guests of another persuasion are sharing our meal.*

'*My husband and I have always taught our children not to pray for too long—they should not get tired—but to pray often. And any opportunity serves for that. . . .*

4

'If we see a street accident, our immediate reaction is to say a Hail Mary for everyone concerned, including the policeman who has to handle the situation.

'The first flowers are out in the garden: a short prayer of thanks. And I silently add a special intention: Let me not be cross if they get trampled underfoot in the little ones' games!

'We hear from a friend who is away: a short prayer for him.

'One of our friends and acquaintances is ill, another is sitting an examination, or expecting a baby, or facing a particularly important decision: all are occasions to pray together for him or her. What prayer? Just a Hail Mary. For we teach our children to love the Holy Virgin.

'We look for opportunities amid the bustle of daily life.

'And here is the text of the prayer we use in our home (my husband composed it at the time of our engagement): "Lord God, who art Father of all men, Son of our Mother, and Spirit of love, fill our human hearts with the infinite desire to possess thee. Bring our love to fruitfulness by the warmth of thy grace, so that our affection, which has its origin in a tangible beauty, may in us and our children flower into a prefiguration of thine eternal glory." '

I feel I must include a long letter here, sent me by a woman who has been responsible for the education of countless girls, at home, at school, and in youth movements:

'I need not enumerate here the qualities that every mother should possess; they can be found in every text-book on the family or home education. To us, what my own mother has been to us speaks infinitely more clearly.

'Mother was widowed while I was still a child. She it was who not only saved the unity of our home, but did most to consolidate and deepen it. She kept alive in her children the *memory of their father. The portrait she drew for them was of a good and God-fearing man who loved his children tenderly, but loved God even more. From our earliest childhood, Mother talked to us about the life to come. Every night at bedtime she said: "Now children, we are one day nearer heaven, where God and Daddy are waiting for us." We often used to go to the cemetery, and Mother talked to us there not about death but about the happiness prepared for us in heaven. She used no childish figures of speech, but told us of the infinite goodness of God, his majesty and his splendour that we shall contemplate in eternity. Through the parables and quotations from the New Testament, Mother introduced us to the Gospel very early. On the day of my brother's first High Mass she wrote beneath the big photograph of Daddy: "Heaven shares our joy", this was her way of reminding us that Daddy was amongst us on this memorable day, and in heaven he shared our joy, because his son was a priest for ever.*

'The eschatological outlook that our mother instilled in us never cast the slightest shadow on our childhood happiness. We never felt it was a reason for sadness. On the contrary, I have always felt very close to heaven, where an infinitely good Father has his dwelling, and where my father had already gone to live. Wasn't that a matter for joy even in this world?

'Mother drew from her faith the strength she needed to bear tribulations, and she was not spared these. Some of her words and actions are still deeply graven on my memory, because they were in no way a pose, but the expression of profoundly Christian convictions.

'I remember how brave she was at the time of Daddy's death. She was left with six children, the oldest 18 and the youngest scarcely two. She toiled for her children with the conviction that God was at her side and she could have un-

shakeable trust in him. Another very heavy blow was the death of my brother, the priest, who was drowned at the age of 30 in an attempt to save one of the boys in his charge in camp. It was then that we several times heard on her lips these words, which send a shiver down me: "Let us say: Yes, Father, again. The Lord has asked us for what we held most precious; if we love him, we ought to be able to give it to him. If the Lord were to say to me: 'I give you back your son, though I would rather keep him beside me,' I would answer: 'Lord, if that is your wish, keep my son, he is yours.' " — These words are typical of my mother's heroism at the tragic time of the death of her dear son, the priest. On the evening of the funeral, when we were all in tears as we sat together, she showed herself the bravest of us all: "Children, don't cry, your brother is happy with the Lord. Now he will always be there with Daddy to help us. Be brave! This new trial proves how much the Lord loves us."

'*In life we must learn to say: "Yes, Father." That was what Mother told us over and over again.*

'*Words like this are not for her the expression of a kind of stoicism or fatalism. There is nothing flabby or apathetic or even phlegmatic about her character. No, she is a saintly and sensitive woman, who derives all her courage from the Lord. Only a few weeks ago, she told me: "I may be well off, but I should have been very unfortunate if I had not had Christ. How grateful I am to my parents for having taught me above all things to fear God." She still often talks with much filial piety of her own father, who from his youth onwards never let a single day go by without praying that the Lord would let him die on a Good Friday, and who on Good Friday 1930 had his dearest wish granted: he was happy to die on that day, hoping to share in Christ's resurrection too.*

'*Mother taught us to pray both in joy—and then her theme was: "We must thank the Lord"—and in adversity —and then our prayers ended with the words: "Thy will be done."*

'*She taught us too to open our hearts to the love of God, and to respond joyfully to the invitations of grace. She taught us to love each other, to thank God for all his gifts, and to say "Yes, Father" even when he asked what cost us most. . . .*

'*That is the synthesis of the religious upbringing she gave us. I should go on for many more pages if I wrote down everything we owe her in that sphere. Yet she was always ready to adapt herself to new situations, and she never kept us on a leading-string. We could travel, accept invitations and invite friends ourselves; above all, we could devote ourselves to Catholic Action activities. She helped us to get ready for our camps and excursions. "If you never forget God in everything you do," she used to say, "you will be all right."*

'*I could spread myself too on her teaching talents as a wife and mother, but what I feel was outstanding and am most grateful for is the Christian education she gave us. Not that I imagine Mother has no faults and can do nothing wrong; but I can make allowances because for me she is always the type of the loving and unselfish mother.*

'*If only our young mothers would realise that there is no better guarantee of their children's happiness than a sound and careful religious upbringing, and that in this field example is worth infinitely more than eloquence!*

'*My students sometimes complain: "I'd like to pray, but I can't. Mother never taught me. She never prays herself. It's hard on me."—or: "Pray? . . . Mother hasn't any time for praying. She hasn't time for me either, she would rather go out to work to buy us nice clothes. But what's the good of nice clothes if she isn't much of a mother to me?"*

'I have never come across a student who regretted the sound religious education she received from her mother. Only once did I hear a pupil complain that evening prayers at home went on and on, with a thousand and one special intentions! But do not some complaints spring less from dislike of religion than from the justifiable desire for a revival of spiritual life? Obviously parents should avoid a surfeit of religion for their children, though not many can complain of this! What girls far more often complain of is their mother's lack of piety. Many mothers nowadays feel the need for prayer less than did the generation before them whose life was much harder; but why do they not teach their children to thank the Lord for all the good things they enjoy?

'The mother is chiefly responsible for the religious climate of the home; households where she is in full agreement with her husband over this are doubly fortunate.

'It is for the mother to interrupt the television programme tactfully and suggest to her husband and children that it is time for the evening prayer. If the programme is an interesting one she must see that prayers are said at some other time. And it is for her too to choose a religious broadcast at the right moment. She must also see that the whole family shares in the Eucharist regularly, and makes use of the sacrament of penance.

'That is what the father expects of the mother, and the children too—implicitly, while they are small. But as they grow up, they will reproach their mother openly if she has not come up to their expectations. If she neglects this side of her responsibilities in the home, the children's chances of a happy life diminish accordingly. In some cases the mother may be the cause of real neuroses in her children because *her daughters (my experience does not extend to boys, but with them too there must be similar cases) are left without support from religion, and sink into an existentialist state of distress or into complete apathy. Just as a starving man reaches the point when he cannot take food though it is his only chance of survival, so children like this realise that nothing except religion can save them. But they are spiritually undernourished, and no longer have strength to save themselves, either on the religious or the psychological level. They hold their mother responsible for their nervous tension, if she has really not known from their earliest childhood how their deepest religious aspirations can be met.'*

FAMILY PRAYER

It is not enough for father, mother and children to lead individual lives of prayer. They must also bring God their collective praise, thanksgiving and supplication. Christ dwells among them, in the home. They must unite themselves with him consciously and so to speak constantly, so that in all circumstances they may be able to say with the same love, Abba, Father.

'Our home,' writes an architect, 'is deeply happy because it lives and flowers in the love of Christ. We are conscious that our marriage is for each of us a vocation, a call to total self-giving to the other. We have come into contact with the "Focolarini" movement, and they have helped us to understand that "where there are two or three gathered together in his name, there is Jesus in the midst of them". So we try to live with Jesus amongst us, like a little cell of the living Church. We share our happiness with our children, who are getting ready to go out into life completely fearlessly!'

'One last point I would like to touch on,' writes a young correspondent, 'is family prayers. I well remember that when I was a child we all said our evening prayers together every day. Now I am 18, and there is nothing left of all that. We never pray now. There was a time when I didn't mind: that sort of thing seemed a waste of time. But I have altered. I look to my home for support I can't find there. Prayer, reading the Scriptures—that is what I should like to bring back into our family. Nowadays they provide the support and certainty I can't do without.

'I am sure, Monsignor, that you are concerned with situations like this, for I feel a solution is possible if only parents and children will talk to each other openly and honestly.'

*   *   *

In what form should we bring this life of family prayer into being?

Christians say grace together before and after meals. So far as possible they all take part together in the divine Feast, the celebration of the Eucharist; if one is prevented, the others are eager to represent him. When things are going well they come together to thank God. And they meet at the bedside of a sick or dying member. Every day is brought to its close by an intimate ceremony in the home: evening prayer and part of the holy Rosary. Speaking of prayers recited together, a mother writes:

'If sharp words have passed during the day, prayer smoothes away irritation and re-establishes good relations. It brings our hearts together and makes them one. Through prayer everything acquires new and deeper significance. When God is with you, everything is smooth and easy.'

And she adds: 'Mothers must give a modern sound to prayer.' Indeed a mother must sometimes ask herself whether the prayers her family uses are not too traditional in form, if they are well enough adapted to the attitude of modern youth and their style in religious matters. In another letter these points are made:

'The problem has different facets. Prayer evokes eternal things, that is, things situated outside us. So it is fitting that human languages when applied to the highest things should have a kind of timeless character. But we must also renew the Word, whose meaning is inexhaustible. Reverence, good taste, and the "supernaturalness" of inspiration will work miracles here, and stop mothers from using expressions too impregnated with the atmosphere of the times. Their love of God will see that they do not fail in this, the most delicate of all their tasks: to find a mode of religious expression which is sufficiently "with it" and yet worthy of the object of its worship.'

In this field of family prayer, nothing is more valuable than variety and personal initiative. Each member of the family must consider how to make the ceremony as significant and as expressive as possible. Each in turn should draw up the programme for it. The reading of a psalm, a song learnt in a youth club, a passage of Scripture, the Creed repeated by all present, or a prayer taken from some book of prayers, a passage from the Liturgy of the Mass or the sacraments, and so on. . . . And it is a good thing if each can mention his own special intentions.

There is no fear of disunity in a home which prays together. Prayer is the best guarantee of the union of hearts and souls. Amid all difficulties, a home like this remains one in Christ, for *its union is brought about at a point infinitely above the causes of dissensions and divisions.* In the climate of these homes, parents and children can say with St Paul: 'For in one Spirit were we all baptised into one body; and in one Spirit we have all been made to drink. And, if one member suffer anything, all the members suffer with it; or, if one member glory, all the members rejoice with it.' (I Cor. 13, 26).

5

Safeguards of the Family

The aim of our inquiry, and of all the action we have taken for the family, is apostolic. We wanted to show what we Christians, together with all our brethren of good will, could and should do in the society of today, to preserve spiritual values and in particular a sound conception of family life. With the help of your replies, I began by drawing up a list of the dangers which threaten the home in present conditions. Then I summarised your opinions on how family life should be conceived and realised if it is to be the source of fervent and fruitful Christian life, and of deep, intense human happiness. So we have established and clearly defined the means by which Christians can help society to resolve the crisis that the institution of marriage is now going through.

THE MISSION OF LEADERS

It is very difficult for married couples to grasp fully the meaning of their faithfulness and to respect the conditions essential for the unity of their homes, when the inspiration of all public life and the whole social order is the desire for domination, cupidity, and the unrestrained pursuit of pleasure. Moreover, how can we instil respect for unselfish love and true faithfulness into young people, if the whole body of science and techniques pursue only their own ends, without a thought for the human soul, and if the prevailing wind that blows through society is egoism, resentment and aggressiveness, if public opinion is contaminated by unworthy forms of publicity and drowned in a flood of childish, materialistic representations of sexuality? The whole of society must react. In the field that concerns us here, the mission and responsibilities of those who wield influence and hold positions of authority are particularly heavy. Of course laws and regulations can be no substitute for the sense of individual responsibility. But without concerted action and organised campaigns it would be idle to hope for any improvement in the situation.

It is obvious that in a society so deeply divided on the ideological plane all this raises some very serious problems. And yet it is essential to be able to count on the collaboration of everyone, a collaboration based on a value that transcends all divisions. And this value can only be respect for human personality. The civil laws must recognise and guarantee the stability of marriage, as both a norm and an ideal. If to safeguard the rights of the individual they make provision for divorce, we must recognise and accept all the consequences of this. Exceptional cases where divorce is justified must be carefully delimited, and every care taken to respect the welfare of the partners, the children and society alike.

Public opinion must be protected at all costs from unscrupulous publicity and its abuses, to which human dignity is completely sacrificed the moment there is any question of commercial profit. The use of leisure must be better regulated. Christian families must make their voice heard—and hope that it will be understood—in a demand that films, sound and television programmes be cleansed of everything that compromises reverence for marriage, the noble conception of love, and respect for human personality. Without any question, broadcasts which constitute an attack on human quality, on *spiritual civilisation*, would disappear if the families that feel strongly about them took joint action instead of complaining in isolation.

I speak now, in the name of countless families who are suffering or feel themselves in danger, to Catholic intellectuals. I earnestly beg them to examine thoroughly the situation I have described. It is for them to find out what should be done to purify this noxious atmosphere. From the Church's point of view, the protection of the institution of the family is a task that falls directly on the laity. No one who has the necessary talents from God, or is entrusted with important office in the political or social field, can remain inactive. What good is it to encourage material progress or provide better housing conditions, *if the family itself is allowed to disintegrate?* And is it not obvious to everyone that a home left to itself cannot escape this terrible danger? The *panem et circenses* which lost Rome will destroy our western civilisation too if our natural leaders do not take concerted action and devise more effective measures. Here is a field in which all men of good will can work together in the spirit of the encyclical *Pacem in terris*, whatever their ideology and philosophic position.

THE MISSION OF SOCIETIES AND HOMES

The home needs help. On the one hand many homes are in danger; on the other, a great many married people have a growing desire to deepen the real foundations of their union, considered and given expression in their lives as a particular form of human and Christian vocation. A double mission, and a very important one, falls on the whole community.

Homes in distress must be able to get immediate help and advice in emergency. In this order of ideas we must mention the already existing *Catholic Marriage Advisory Councils*. Teams of specialists are ready in these centres to help homes with problems touching on the harmony between husband and wife or family.

It is unfortunately a fact that most unhappy homes consult them only when the evil is beyond cure. Help and advice can be provided on a generous and effective scale only if the emergency quota is not greatly exceeded. Husband and wife ought to find advice and assistance in the ordinary difficulties of married life. Marriage councils should set about organising themselves as a sort of first-aid service.

An increasing number of homes should be given the necessary training so that they may bring this fraternal 'first-aid' to other homes, for what belongs to their natural setting must be preferable to anything taken on by a 'substitute organism'. Under the direction of competent advisers, carefully chosen homes could perfectly well be incorporated in Marriage Councils and share their activities, as is done in many countries in Europe and America. The more effectively preparation for marriage is organised, the better will happy homes be able to take charge of homes in distress. Then specialist help will be needed only for difficult or obviously pathological cases. In any event this must be a condition of the successful solution of today's 'crisis of growth' in the family. It would be absurd and contrary to the order of things to rely exclusively on specialists. There are too few of them, and they are fully employed on the difficult cases they have to resolve. Certainly, what is needed if we are to take action of any scope and real efficacy is 'first aid' brought to homes by homes.

Great stress has already been laid on the importance of the mission that falls on homes, not only to help in the way we have just discussed, but in many other activities, and especially in courses of preparation for marriage. All this obviously presupposes a common effort directed to the suitable training of what I shall call 'evangelising homes'.

A deep and dynamic spiritual life must be developed with the help of well-informed priests. So the ethics of married life will benefit from the revival which has in the last few years been noticeable in Christian ethics in general.[1] To this end, it is essential that the real foundations of Christian life in marriage are presented in a *positive way*. Starting from these basic principles, married couples can then aim at a spirituality which is suited to the stage they have reached in their sacramental life, and which they have of their own free will taken on themselves.

But this spirituality must lie close to ordinary life and always be both explicitly Christian and profoundly human. Marriage, by virtue of its sacramental character, must be recognised as a path to holiness for husband and wife. The full flowering of natural love is one of its essential aspects. We must appeal to the homes themselves, for their experience is indispensable in bringing us to a sharper awareness of the conditions for this fulfilment. And we must make sure too that we do not stray from the direct line of Christian doctrine and tradition; that is why the co-operation of the priest is essential here.

*　　*　　*

Praiseworthy efforts have already been made in the direc-

---

[1] I refer my readers here to the authoritative work of Paul Anciaux, *Le Sacrement du mariage - Aux sources de la morale conjugale* (ed. Nauwelaerts, Louvain), in which I have more than once found inspiration in writing this report.

tion we have indicated, and it is worth noting in some detail the forms they have taken.

The *Equipes Notre-Dame* (Teams of Our Lady) are made up of small teams of four to eight homes, which on the basis of the 'rule' of the movement help each other to bring the spirit of the Gospel into their whole life and encourage husband and wife to strive for perfection in conjugal life. They meet monthly to pray, discuss some family problem, studied at home beforehand, and to pool their problems and worries. Every other year the members of each team make a short retreat together.

The *Family Groups, Christian Family Movement Groups,* and *Family and Social Apostolate Groups* are 'forums' for ten or so young households, who declare themselves ready to make a united effort towards a genuinely Christian life, in line with the Church's teaching on marriage and with pedagogic principles. They exchange the results of their experience and thought.

A home affiliated to one of these movements undertakes to attend, husband and wife together, the monthly meetings arranged for the year; to attend Mass, either on the day of the meeting or the following day, and once every week, as far as this is possible; to pray every day as a family; to take part once a year in a day of recollection for families.

THE MISSION OF ALL

Formerly society was far less complex than now. Its limits were narrower and thus much closer together, and they provided a support for the family. The whole of life, at least in our own regions, was imbued with the spirit of natural law and Christian principles. Today things are very different. Far more than formerly, a *personal* attitude and a *personal* choice is required of everyone. Everyone therefore must be able to benefit by a training which teaches him to shoulder his own responsibilities. And everyone must have the opportunity to discover for himself the beauty of a morally sound family life, so that he may dedicate himself in all freedom to this ideal.

Public authorities and responsible bodies must take appropriate action, as we have said. But it must be clearly recognised that at this juncture it is less a question of enforcing rules and regulations than of persuading individuals to undertake the proper exercise of their liberty.

In their preparation for family and conjugal life young people must acquire reasoned convictions, based on the teaching of the Church. But homes too need help. Nowadays married people are no better prepared than youth to enter into a personal engagement. Public morality has collapsed almost without warning. Suddenly adultery and unfaithfulness in marriage, free love and profligacy are flaunted in the full light of day in our towns and villages, and have come to be considered almost normal procedure. Adults were taken unawares. They were ill prepared to make a personal stand. They were not yet taking responsibility for their own lives. In other words, they were not wholly adult. They must complete their apprenticeship in their trade of living like men.

*   *   *

Who will give young people and adults this chance to complete their human and Christian education? The Church of Jesus Christ has here a mission of cardinal importance, the mission of presenting the principles and energies that she holds from her divine Founder in a form suited to the needs of the times. The Church intends to fulfil this mission. This is the sole aim of the Ecumenical Council. But what exactly will be the decisions of the Council in the field that concerns us here?

Many of the faithful, either from force of habit or from an inferiority complex, will say at once: 'The Council will tell the members of the clergy what they are to preach and put in train in homes and educational societies. . . .' Certainly the Council will give instructions touching the apostolate of priests. But is that really the most important and specific aspect of the Second Vatican Council? Of course not! All the indications are that the Council will declare emphatically that Christian husbands and wives must *themselves,* in the first instance, collaborate in the 're-education' of the home. No one doubts that there is urgent need for the Church to organise herself for the rescue of the family as an institution. But the Council will say to all the faithful: 'You, Christians— you are the Church, you are God's people.'

To all Christians who have received the sacrament of matrimony the Council will say, and say over and over again: 'Through the sacrament you have received, you have been given a mandate, in Christ and in his Church, not only to provide adequate preparation for marriage for your sons and daughters, but also to reach out in brotherhood to other homes.' By virtue of the sacrament of matrimony, every Christian home is responsible for the others, and has the mission to help them to bring intensively into their lives, in the difficult circumstances we know all too well, the message of peace and joy that Christ brought us.

Indeed, the faithful must constantly call to mind that through their baptism they share in the redemptive death and resurrection of Christ. Their incorporation in Christ is a conscious and generous sharing in the life and mission of Christ who perpetuates himself in his Church. Baptism finds its complement and its fulfilment in the sacrament of matrimony. Marriage is a covenant by which husband and wife bind themselves to help Christ in his Church.

The intimacy of husband and wife in no way means isolation or 'egoism for two'. A married couple does not receive the grace of Christ that they may shut themselves up in an ivory tower, or make a little island of Christian happiness for themselves alone. Marriage is a sign of the covenant between God and man. It is the symbol of the union of Christ and the Church. That is why marriage is a vocation to fruitful love, to an effective sharing in the creative work of God and the redemptive work of Jesus among men. The more important is the help that husband and wife receive from Christ for their growth in mutual love and faithfulness, the more pressingly does he urge them to work together with him, as a family, to the glory of God and the salvation of other homes.

Love of God and love of one's neighbour are the two essential and complementary poles of Christian married life. It is in their capacity as maker of a home that Christian husbands and wives must be apostles. They must consider as a mission which God entrusts to them in particular the Christian community's task of helping homes in difficulty.

'The whole question,' writes the father of six children, 'is whether a home can be truly happy if it retires within itself and never feels itself responsible for the misery of other homes, and if the happiness of other families is not its constant care. Surely true happiness lies in being open to others, in exercising charity as widely as possible. Often nothing more is needed to put a home back on the right road than the radiant example of another and happy home. But the most efficacious help of all comes from personal contacts between homes. Such contacts can be established in various ways: within the organisations and movements one belongs to,

through professional activities, in the course of the thousand and one little occurrences, happy or sad, that can bring families together.

'*Every opportunity to say a pleasant word must be taken. That simple word prepares the ground for a more intimate conversation. It is through the ordinary relations of friendship that we learn best how to know and resolve the difficulties of other people. It is the ideal way to act as intermediary and to pass on difficult cases to the only people who can provide effective help.*'

Happiness is infectious

I am convinced that many Christian families underestimate the influence they might exercise. Several letters include among the ways that light may spread 'the sight of someone else's happiness . . . that attractive force of true joy . . . the example of a profoundly happy family life . . . the possibility of infecting people round about one with happiness'.

Since we have been publishing some of the replies to our inquiry in our parish magazines, several correspondents say that they have found the reading of these simple testimonies a real stimulus.

'*I never knew,' writes a husband, 'that there were so many happy homes. It surprised and encouraged me. I must admit that in the last two years I had grown very pessimistic and was often very depressed. I had got to the point of wondering whether there were still homes where the teaching of the Church was taken seriously, and was something more than just idealism or theory. . . . You can't imagine how much good these letters did me! My wife has already said: "The parish magazine must be an extraordinarily good paper, for you're much nicer when you've read it!" She is sitting beside me*

*now, and whispering in my ear: "Yes, write all that, and say
that we thank God for the happiness of other families: it
makes us happy too." '*

A teacher writes:

'*Every week my wife and I read these fine and often very
moving letters. They do us good. When we read testimonies
like these, we are encouraged to model our own conduct on
them. This Lent our family life has improved in many ways.
More than once we have said to ourselves: "If other people
do this, why shouldn't we too?"*

'*They have taught us a lesson, too. We have learnt how a
home can be uplifted and encouraged by seeing and hearing
how life goes on in happy homes. Nowadays there are so
many bad examples to be seen in the papers, films, and everyday life. A man who is not prepared is often taken in by all
this; he models his own life on what he finds in the cinema,
literature or the press.*

' "*Good people*" *don't make a show of their daily life, and
one is reluctant to tell others what goes on at home, for
example in the sphere of religion, and so too often mischief-
makers have it all their own way. The publication of these
letters of witness is really well-timed.*

'*It is time for us to proclaim proudly the sound Christian
traditions that govern life in so many deeply Christian homes.
Monsignor, let us have a fine "family album", which will
show us the marvels of God's love on every page. That would
make many married people think. It is time for a revival of
respect for good homes. In our villages, only the ones which
are no longer good get talked about!'*

Coming out of our ivory tower

A lighted candle should not be put under a bushel, but on

a candlestick. That is a theme for all Christian homes to meditate. An attitude of isolation and neutrality would be a kind of betrayal of the faithful. Their vocation is to bear witness to the Lord. The simple revelation of what they think and do could have a salutary influence on so many homes! Quite apart from any discussion and any attempt to bring waverers back to the fold, the mere existence of happy homes, really living by the sacraments, is enough to produce a real revolution in the families round about them. Provided, as we said, that they do not retreat within themselves and live in isolation. That is of fundamental importance. A truly Christian home will only be a beacon for families in distress if the principles that inspire their thought and conduct can be clearly seen in their daily life. The members of such a household must strive to live simply 'among men', without pose or affectation. Theirs will be a bright and light-giving house. We repeat what one of our correspondents has said: 'It is through the ordinary relations of friendship that we learn best how to know and resolve the difficulties of other people.' This is profoundly true. We must avoid artificiality, and the best way to do this is to share fully in the conditions of life of those around us.

Cold, artificial, inhuman, un-Christian—how else can we describe the conduct of many Catholics who refuse to become involved in relationships of cordial brotherly friendship with families in the same neighbourhood, or people they rub shoulders with every day in the office or factory? Christians with no flame of love, dried-up business men, frivolous society women or silly little girls, who have none of the simple, sincere, heedful kindness of Christ who dwells in them and who desires, through them, to be the Church of all men, and above all of the weak and the humble.

A Christian home must live 'organically', like a living cell of the great family of the faithful. It can only serve as a light for those round about in so far as it establishes relations of true friendship with them. A home is respected and loved by others, and wins their affection and trust, only if it shows them spontaneous kindness and sympathy. Outward forms that reflect inward virtues kindle in others sympathy and interest for the Christian life to which they bear witness.

Catholic educational organisations are making a very praiseworthy effort in this direction. In many cases the influence of these movements has enabled sound ideas on family life to win and keep a footing with their members. The reading of their publications, attendance at their meetings, and above all home visiting by their responsible leaders, play an extremely important part. Many families owe the strength and quality of their union to the training husband and wife received, or are still receiving, in the Catholic Action or similar movements.

A leader of the Action Sociale Féminine Chrétienne (Women's Christian Social Action) movement writes on this subject: 'If only we who have been fighting for years in the ranks of the Social Action movement could tell you all the good our leaders are doing in their own homes and the homes of their members! The training they have had in study-groups, meetings, retreats, and so on, gives them strength and grace for this work. Often their homes are the support of the weak and depressed in their neighbourhood. They should indeed encourage still more good homes to share their happiness with the less happy. There is no dearth of opportunity for full use of the talents the Divine Master spoke of.'

Christ in the neighbourhood

Here we must say a word about the part that the society

known as STRADA can and should play in the drive to restore the values of family life. This movement of mutual aid and apostolate is centred on the locality, and designed to equip the community of the parish with a new structure adapted to modern needs; its mission is to renew the life of the locality.

The fundamental idea of STRADA is the notion of *proximity*, from the Latin *proximus*, meaning *neighbouring, next*, or *near*. Near in space? Certainly, in its first sense. But it is a property of human life to add a spiritual 'dimension' to the values of space and time. The man who lives *near* me, topographically speaking, has things in common with me that others have not; I know him better than a man living in a district further off. If there were some natural catastrophe, or some human error destroyed your street, or your district, the real interdependence which links you all would at once become apparent, and your effective and active solidarity would be brought into action. And so on: there are many bonds between those who live in the same corner of the world. The first social unit is the couple, the family; in many respects, the street comes next, the locality, the 'block', as they say in the great cities of America.

In the life of the parish, the locality is a specific element with its own character and customs, its own ways of 'taking part'. It must be a living cell of the parochial organism, a cell made up of men living side by side in this life on earth. These men must not spy on each other, criticise and envy each other, but know, love and help one another in the charity of Christ.

I appeal to you again to carry on resolutely the movement STRADA has undertaken in this spirit. It is an excellent way for Christian families to become in all humility the 'salt of the earth' and 'light of the world'.

Another family expresses their opinion that

'there is no determining cause to break up homes if they have sufficient support in the accomplishment of their mission. They should find this support in the priests who visit them regularly, and in friends, neighbours, those who are near. STRADA must continue its effort of thought and its plan of action to strengthen still further the solidarity between neighbours. Why should not families in the same street, or the same section of a street, meet from time to time in the house of one family which would act as host, to study and discuss some problem of family life in a Christian spirit? Experience has already shown that meetings like this are a real blessing for some homes.'

'A happy home,' think another couple, *'spreads a beneficial sort of infection round about it. You must lay constant stress on the importance of the life of the locality. Centred as it is on this reality, STRADA must persevere. The more friendship and help unite families among themselves, the more a convinced Christian household, practising what it preaches, will bring all other homes closer to Christ.'*

Another correspondent notes: 'It will perhaps be years before the first tangible results can be seen. We must not lose hope, but must each find strength in his faith to persevere in this form of apostolate, and gradually gain the confidence of others. If a home in our neighbourhood is passing through a time of crisis, we must pray God to enlighten and uphold them, keep in contact with them by little attentions, and take advantage of the smallest family happenings to show our sympathy. On occasion the charitable neighbour will confide some aspect of his own family life, to show that one can always count on the help of Heaven, through the sacrament of matri-

mony. And so little by little confidence will be born. On both sides there will be more frankness and openness. It is when a household has deserved and won the friendship of neighbouring families in these ways that God's hour may strike, the hour when one receives confidences that really matter, when one can do lasting good and perhaps even save a family.'

The art of communication

When an atmosphere of friendship and trust has been born of contacts such as these, Christian husbands and wives can, by the spoken word, fulfil their mission as collaborators with Jesus Christ: *Dei adjutores*. Who, in all conscience, could claim that he does his duty well enough by simply adopting a kindly, modest attitude, without making use of the gift of 'communicating' by speech which the Creator entrusted to him? Speech is an art. There is an effective way of expressing thought and an ineffective way. There is a way of *serving* and a way of *betraying* in speech. Fellow Christians, for most of us self-examination would not be out of place at this point, and especially for those whose calling lays on them the duty of talking to others.

A diocesan writes:

'What aberration so often causes Christians who are really concerned with their responsibilities to neglect the primary art of talking about the truth in a way worthy of truth? Whoever reverences the object he is speaking of writing about is reluctant to speak or write about it unworthily. Whoever ardently desires the end, desires the means. To serve an idea, to defend a position, to "bear witness" profitably, one must learn the art of setting out, analysing, proving and refuting, the art of unlocking hearts, the art of sowing the seeds of life

*in them, the art of convincing and persuading—the ABC of
the apostolate, but an ABC, alas, too often forgotten.'*

To work then, my brethren, all you who are eager to talk
well of Christ, to implant a little charity, a little truth, in so
many hungry souls to whom the modern world in fact offers
very little in spite of all its tawdry glitter.

Every day the press, radio, television, magazines, records,
etc., communicate with adults, young people, and children.
What do they say? Are their words the words of life or of
death? wholesome words or poisoned? Listen carefully to the
voices raised in this so-called Christian nation. You can hear
that they are not Christian words; in general this is a vast
betrayal, a betrayal that is tolerated, that is not counter-
balanced by the voice of true Christians. We are collaborators
with the Word of God, we carry Christ within us, the living
Word. Can we keep silence? 'We cannot but speak the things
which we have seen and hear,' said the Apostles (Acts 4,
20). Shall we not speak them? shall we not *learn* to speak
them?

The lesson is a difficult one, there is no disguising. It is
easier to scoff at moral values than to defend them. It is
easier to insinuate doubts than to inspire faith. It is harder
to express what goes on in the inmost soul than frivolous
things. We are often called to the difficult duty of sacrificing
a certain reticence, and reposing a great deal of confidence in
someone else, so as to obtain a very little from him.

There is much talk nowadays, in utilitarian relations, of
what is called the technique of persuasion: business men,
trade representatives, public relations officers, insurance
agents, buyers and sellers, all are trained in the art of conversing and convincing. And will not all you Christian husbands and wives train yourselves in the art of talking to your

neighbour? the supreme and delicate art of never giving pain, of mingling charity with the outspokenness that is often called for? Will you not learn the difficult art of being at the disposal of another, being present to another, so that every moment he feels that because he is your brother in Christ, but also because he is himself and no one else, he is getting and holding all your attention, all your friendship?

You can learn everything nowadays. Except perhaps, how to communicate with another without betraying your message. The time has come when that will seem barbarous. And above all we must learn without more delay—for the rising generations clamour for urgent measures—how to talk to young people, to understand and respect the youth of young people, to touch the conscience of the young, to respond to the insatiable demands of souls thirsty for life, life in the measure of man—of the man of today, not of yesterday. Speaking very generally, the older generation have been very clumsy in their relationships with young people these last few years. The specific qualities of modern youth have, I believe, gone unrecognised. We call on Christian families to make a great effort of understanding and love to rectify that at the first possible moment.

Read a passage from this little book every evening, and so as to train yourselves in the art of conversing and bearing witness, talk it over among yourselves for a few minutes. I assure you that very soon you will have acquired great facility in the art of holding an evangelising conversation. In these conversations the important thing is not so much to refute objections. Rather say simply what you do so as to get to know each other better, to put up with each other's failings, to help each other and especially to respect your partner's individuality. Express the confidence you have in Divine Providence amid all difficulties and trials, and speak of the consolation that your faith rains down on your sorrows. That will be *your* way of spreading the *good news*, the way to which the Lord calls you.

* * *

At the end of this long pastoral letter I take my leave of you, my dear people. The Master has entrusted to you the fundamental task of forming a *cell of the Church*, '*ecclesiola*', as the Fathers called it. But he has entrusted to you as well a mission to homes which have not the same faith, to suffering homes, worried homes.

Let the Christian conception of family life be known through your conversations, let the testimony of your Christian home be seen by the whole world. Above all, stay closely united with the Lord who bound himself to you at your marriage. Through your life and conversation men will realise that the simplicity of the Gospel hides a wonderful and divine strength. And when you leave them, they will have seen the Lord Jesus through you. Like the disciples of Emmaus long ago, when they recognised the person of Christ, they will say: 'Was not our heart burning within us whilst he spoke in the way and opened to us the scriptures?'